Lt. Col. C. C. Jamison (handwritten signature)

MEMORIES
FROM TUSKEGEE

SGT James J. Irwin SR (handwritten)
477th MED, BOMB G.P. (handwritten)

The Life Story of
Lieutenant Colonel Clarence C. Jamison

As told to

James Christ

ISBN 0-9788604-0-3

Published by
Tuskegee Leader LLC

2006

1518 E. 12th St.
Casa Grande, AZ.
85222

Printed in the United States of America by
Mosaic Press LLC, PO Box 436
Happy Camp, CA.

Contents

Preface

Although names, dates and places have been thoroughly checked, this book makes no claim to be a historical text. Instead, my memoirs produce the events and experiences of a young black American during an era that changed the United States of America and, really, the world.

Though this book chronicles my eighty-eight year life, the Second World War is the backdrop. I have tried to draw memories of all of my wartime experiences-- pleasant, humorous, serious, and sad-- to give an accurate depiction of what life was like in the 99th Pursuit Squadron. The time spent in this elite group of men is without a doubt the best, and worst, times in my life. It is also that which I am most proud to have belonged.

This book shows how when given the opportunity, every member of our nation, regardless of race, creed, color or gender, is an invaluable asset to our country's strength and growth. It also relates how difficult it was for black Americans to be able to do their part and how racial injustices actually hampered the efforts of our great country sixty years ago.

I would like to thank James Christ for doing such a superb job capturing my thoughts and putting them to paper. Of all my interviews, James has portrayed my thoughts and personal experiences better than anyone. He has the rare ability to accurately write someone else's perspective. James did such an outstanding job I allowed him to write my memoirs.

And finally, my thanks are due to all the original members of the 99th Pursuit Squadron who shared with me the wonderful and exciting times as pioneers in military aviation as well as the frustrating injustices of segregation. Also, I would like to give a special thanks to those men at Tuskegee who did not become pilots and were "washed out" of the pilot program without ever having the opportunity - which pilots of other races had - to continue their training in less demanding aircraft.

Letter from the author

I first met Lieutenant Colonel Clarence Jamison in 1998 on a Southwest Airlines flight to Cleveland. He was wearing a Tuskegee Airmen's ball cap and I asked him about it. He was 81 years old then. Now he's 88. He is a strong, yet gentle, proud, yet humble, man of keen intelligence and wit. He is a kind man capable of great endurance even in the winter of his life. To give an example of the fortitude of this remarkable man, the mornings (months apart) before our second and third interviews, he rose at 3:30 am to go to the hospital for his dialysis. All the blood in his body was run through a machine before being pumped back into him. It is an exhausting five-hour procedure. Colonel Jamison then met me for over three hours where he talked of his wartime experiences, remembering dates, names and places. He also went up and down stairs, rummaged through old boxes looking for pictures and records and then went off to have copies and duplicate photo's made. On each occasion, if I didn't have a flight to catch we would have continued.

Colonel Jamison is extremely proud of his family. To see him walk through his spotless home where pictures on the walls are like a shrine to his family and to listen to the pride in his voice as he points to his daughter or granddaughter is something to admire and even envy. But the greatest quality about this man is his wonderful sense of humor. He is laughing and smiling all the time. It was such a pleasant experience and I feel fortunate that he allowed me, of all the many people who offered to write his memoirs, the chance to record his fascinating life.

I would like to thank...

-Sue Stein, PhD, for her help editing this manuscript.

-John Kelley Jr. and Mike White for helping pick the title.

-Ed Blackshear for reading my manuscript and offering constructive criticism.

-A grateful thank you to Jay Templeton, Mike Figueroa, Marty Boetel, Andrew Robles and Athena.

-My father John M. Christ and my brother Joseph Christ.

James F. Christ

GROWING UP, 1918 – 1936

I was born February 25th 1918 in Littlerock, Arkansas, the third son of Richard and Sallie Jamison, a poor, hard-working southern black couple. I was too young to remember, but we lived with my grandparents in a wood shack without electricity or running water. Jobs were hard to find in those days so for a young black couple trying to make their life better in the segregated south, when I was three years old my parents took my siblings, Thurston and Sterling, and moved to Cleveland, Ohio, to find jobs before sending for the rest of us. That was what a poor family had to do in America if they had dreams of making their life better. It was almost two years before I saw my parents again.

My grandparents became my parents. They were good, hard-working, loving people and my sister Rae and I considered them our mom and dad. Finally, my parents sent word that they were ready and my grandparents packed us all in a train and we moved from Little Rock to Cleveland. It was a long, slow trip before we were all together again in one tiny house in Ohio.

A woman I didn't know was overjoyed to see us and ran out to hug everyone. She said she was my mother, but for the last two years it was my grandmother I ran to when I was crying. My mother was very hurt that her own children didn't recognize

5

her and it was made worse each time I called my grandmother "Mom." She even became angry after it happened more than a few times and I had to adjust to calling her that. But she was a loving woman so it didn't take long and soon our family life returned to normal.

I was five when we moved to Ohio and it was quite an adventure because in Cleveland I was sent away to spend my days in this thing called kindergarten. Up until then I had always remained home with my grandmother. Being sent off to school would be the first real memory I would retain throughout the years because it was something so completely foreign. Little Rock was segregated. Cleveland was integrated! I had never been around white people before. Now I was being taught by white teachers and sat beside white children.

I immediately took to school and excelled at it. I got good grades all through elementary school and I enjoyed showing them to my parents, who for some reason were delighted by them. Because it was important to mom and dad, it became important to me. I never played hooky and I always strove to have a perfect report card to show them. Even if I had a cold, I never stayed home, no matter how sick or tired I was. This was not exactly because I didn't want to stay home; it was because my parents said, "Get your butt to school!" It was just understood in the Jamison household that you always went to school and you always did your homework. We had six children in my family and education was a priority my parents demanded of all of us.

My father, Richard Henry Jamison, was a hard worker. He was employed at McKesson and Robbins Wholesale Drug Company. Dad was lucky to have a steady job during the Great Depression. We knew a lot of people who didn't. He always did extra things at his workplace for additional money. Dad was a porter, a clerk; he also did some of the shipping and packing. As a result he could wrap the neatest Christmas packages. My father worked every day and even worked as the weekend night watchman on Sundays to earn extra income. My dad always worked. Because I enjoyed being around him so much, I would take the streetcar down to his workplace to spend Sunday's with him. He never had a chance to go out and play baseball or basketball with us [not like I was able to do with my son in the years to come]. He was too busy trying to feed his family during the Great Depression. So many families went hungry.

I'd follow my dad to numerous stations around the company and watch him punch different time clocks. This was to make sure that at a specific time, a particular area was secure. Being the night watchman, he carried a gun. I thought it was the neatest thing that my father carried a gun. In the late 1920s, nobody carried firearms but police officers so I figured, "Wow, Dad must be important!" I would spend hours with him and we both loved it. I knew my father loved me very much. He loved

7

all his children, but I was a quiet, studious kid who never got in trouble. I think he liked that. I never wanted to disappoint him. My father developed my character. By watching him, I learned to think first, to remain calm, to work hard, and to put priorities and family first.

Because my father worked so much, my mom was the head of our house. Mom always made sure we had a clean home, good meals, and clean clothes. She was a god-fearing, church-going Baptist. The Bible says, "Spare not thy rod on thy children." Mom must have taken that to heart. She whipped the hell out of us with a switch when we crossed the line. To add to the terror, she even made us pick the switch off the tree. She'd whip us on the legs a couple of times and that was enough. Of course, we'd yell like we were being killed. She kept a pretty tight reign on all of us. She was one of the heads of the neighborhood. We lived on 85th Street in Cleveland and back then everyone looked out for each other's children. We had a good community and strong women like my mom were the reason for it. We were always together, playing stickball or some sort of ball game in the street. We didn't have to worry too much about cars back then. That is, until my grandfather let me drive his car.

My Grandfather was a feisty old guy. Where my father was calm and non-confrontational, my grandfather was outspoken and assertive. He had a 1926 Dodge. He taught me how to drive a stick shift. I remember learning how to drive that car when I was thirteen. My father never knew how to drive. He never had the time to learn because he worked so much. My grandfather, though, let me drive up and down the street. Though it was probably illegal, there weren't many restrictions back then and I was a good driver so he trusted me. That was the beginning of my mechanical future.

I'll never forget when my grandfather bought a used 1932 Ford V-8, the first V-8 Ford ever made. It could move. I was fifteen when I first drove it. I used to get that car up to sixty miles per hour on our street. In 1932, that was flying. My grandfather would let me drive it around the block and I'd pile all my friends in and scream down that road. It was a big thrill. There wasn't much traffic so we didn't have to worry much, but it was a fun, wild time, driving that car. That was my first inclination toward machines of speed. Of course, my grandfather never had a clue that I was driving up the street like that. I was a very careful driver, especially when someone was watching. Because my grandfather saw how responsible I was, he'd allowed me to drive my grandmother to church. Otherwise, I didn't go very far.

As a child in Cleveland, I naturally took an interest in flying. The national air races were in Cleveland. We would watch the races whenever we could, just us kids. It was something interesting to do and flying was still so new and

9

fascinating. We would take the street car down to the Cleveland Municipal Airport and watch from outside the gate. You had to pay to get in so we just stood outside and watched. They flew right over us anyway so it wasn't like we were missing out by not being inside. I remember watching a veteran racing pilot named Jimmy Doolittle fly overhead in a GB Speedster. It was fast. He would roar overhead and it was incredible. Jimmy Doolittle was a name that would soon acquire nationwide fame in the coming Second World War.

My parents added two more siblings to the family a few years after we got to Ohio. Richard Henry Jr. and Alvin Rolland came in the mid 1920's. I don't know if any of my brothers were happy with the names my parents picked for them but I wasn't fond of mine. Clarence Clifford! I didn't mind C.C, or even C.J, but I didn't like Clarence. Of course, I was smart enough not to let anyone know that, especially once I got into high school. [i]

In high school, besides having the name Clarence, I was a small guy, thin and short-- all the makings for a kid that would get beat up or bullied. Since I didn't want that to happen or to be classified as a sissy, especially with so many rough guys at our school, I made friends with some of the toughest kids. These friendships all began with a test. Once, I was sitting next to one of the toughest kids in school, and we both knew he wasn't going to pass this test. So I told him not to sign his name

10

or to make a mark on his paper. When the exam began, I finished mine as fast as I could and then when the teacher wasn't looking, I slipped my test over to him; taking his back. I finished it, too, and put my name on it. My friends were amazed that I could finish two tests so quickly. I only had to do this a couple of times before all the toughest guys wanted to be my friends. Of course, I always missed a few answers on their tests so the teacher wouldn't get suspicious while I made sure I got A's, but my friends were more than happy with their B's. Soon, if someone said something smart to me, these guys would step in fast, "Hey, C.J. is my friend. Don't mess with him!"

My parents instantly became concerned when I started to hang out with such rough characters. They wanted me to get new friends before I got into serious trouble or became a juvenile delinquent. It was a rock and a hard place for me. My parents didn't want me hanging around with thugs and I didn't want to get pushed around. I always considered myself too smart to do stupid stuff; and if I did, I was always careful not to get caught, but my parents were still concerned. I rectified the problem by never letting my mom or dad see me with any of the rough crowd. I certainly didn't change my friends though. Keeping the status quo at school was too important. I wanted to make sure that nobody messed with me and having the toughest kids as friends ensured that. I had a lot of guys that I called friends but there was only a handful that I really hung around with. One of them was Bill Brooks. He had a little brother named Sidney who was always tagging along. We used to play basketball, baseball, football, you name it.

That was an enjoyable time in my life. High school was a lot of fun. I enjoyed being one of the best students; the only straight-A male student in my class. There were a few white girls who got A's, too, but they studied constantly. I did not. I was friends with them because all the good students were in the AP (Advanced Placement) classes together. We also took French. There were only a few of us, less than ten, who took French. All these classes and all this studying were to pay off big in later life. When I went to the University of Chicago, the Dean was looking at my transcripts. He was a very well educated man and exceedingly proper. He obviously saw I had taken French all through high school because he started talking to me in French. I threw it back at him so fast his jaw dropped. We conversed in French for the rest of the interview. You see, in high school French class, we never spoke English. Every word was in French. I could tell the dean was impressed. "You don't need to take a foreign language," he said.

THE UNIVERSITY OF CHICAGO, 1936 -1940

When I graduated from high school, it was right off to college. It's interesting because my parents had no education, but recognized it meant everything. They were, of course, proud of me, but they also expected a lot. There was no way their children were not going to college. They scraped and scrounged and went without so that their children could have an education and a future. The University of Chicago was a natural choice for me because I had an uncle who lived in Chicago who I could stay with. He was a doctor. His name was Clarence Edward Jamison and I was his namesake. He lived on 63rd Street, and the campus was on 55th so it was very convenient because I could walk to school. My uncle also helped me with tuition. To show my gratitude, I tried to help out any way I could. My aunt and uncle had one child and I'd baby sit for them. I was 18 and my cousin Rose Mary was 8. She was like my little sister.

College was sort of like kindergarten had been; new, huge, intimidating and white! I was a Bacteriology major and wanted to become a doctor just like my uncle. It was a tough workload with Biology, Chemistry, Anatomy, Zoology and many other subjects, but school always came fairly easy to me. It was a little different to be in a classroom with all white students, though. There weren't many black students at the

University of Chicago so we were naturally drawn together. Everyone smoked back in the 1930's and usually we'd just walk up to someone and bum a cigarette. That's how an introduction would begin. That was how I met my best friend Sherman White of Montgomery, Alabama. There were so few black students at the university that a few of my friends were even graduate students. But it was a fun time. In a place that was very intimidating anyway, we quickly made friends. Most of us joined the same fraternity, Kappa Alpha Psi. That was where I met another friend, Jack Rogers, whom I would later see at Tuskegee.

Looking back on my life, the only doubts I was ever to have were at the University of Chicago. When I enrolled, it was one of the best schools in the country, rated just behind Harvard and a few other Ivy League schools. All of my teachers and almost everyone in my freshman class was white. It was very daunting. I learned real fast that I wasn't as smart as I thought I was. For the first time in my life I had to work like hell. I was having real trouble in my English class and went to talk to the teacher. He was a young white guy, not much older than me. He encouraged me, "Jamison, you can do it. Just apply yourself and try harder." Well, I believed him. He inspired me and I studied twice as hard as I ever had in my life. After the midterm exam, he called me in to his office. I was terrified right up until I entered and saw his grin. He was so proud and so happy that it surprised me. I had gotten the highest grade in the class. That was all I needed. From that point on, I knew I could hold my own with anyone. I became a valedictorian among some of the best students in the country.

Up to that point I was so busy with school that I never had time for a girlfriend. I had a number of female friends that I used to walk to school with but nothing romantic. That is, until I saw Phyllis Louis Piersawl.

Phyllis was from Wyoming, Ohio, a suburb of Cincinnati and she was beautiful! Phyllis was a few months older than me. She'd transferred in from another college when I was a sophomore. It was one of the first days of school, late August, when I saw her. "Hey, who is that?" I asked Sherman, immediately determined to meet her. There was nothing romantic about our first meeting, though. I just walked up and bummed a cigarette off her and that's how we met. Soon we were going out a lot together and spending a lot of time with each other. It wasn't easy at first because dating takes money. I never had much money although she was well off. I was so broke that one time when I wanted to take her to a fraternity dance but didn't have the cash to buy her a corsage, I asked my buddy Hubert White (no relation to Sherman White) if I could borrow the money. Since I lived with my uncle and he already helped with tuition, I hated asking him to buy anything. He already did so much. Well, when I asked Hubert, he didn't have any money, either. He had to pawn his only suit to come up with enough cash for me to buy the corsage. Hubert was a good friend.

In 1936 I was eighteen. I enjoyed learning and felt I was well on my way toward a future as a doctor. Now, being at a university, there was a lot of talk around campus about a coming war with both Germany and Japan. By 1938 it looked increasingly likely and I realized war was definitely coming sooner or later. I thought about that and knew I'd probably be drafted into the Army or Navy, something I did not want to happen. The armed forces weren't integrated yet and I knew I would be given some menial duty like a steward or a cook. If I had to go into the military, I wanted to be flying.

President Roosevelt knew the country was heading for war. To prepare for the eventual conflict against Hitler, the defense department had created the Civilian Pilot Training Program, which would increase the future number of pilots for the Army Air Corps and inevitable war. Colleges were encouraged to offer this program. I said to Sherman, "Let's sign up for this pilot training program. It's extra hours toward our degree outside of our major and it looks interesting." I thought it would be fun to fly. Sherman just said, "You know its lily white?" Regardless, we didn't expect any trouble so we went down and enrolled. Sherman and I were the first black students at the University of Chicago to sign up. Around the country

16

there were less than a handful of us from the integrated schools. That right there shows why it was so important to offer the program at black colleges. (Otherwise there would just be a trickle of black pilots from integrated universities.) But the program wasn't offered to all the black schools. There were only six black colleges in the entire United States to even offer the program. It would be these pilots who would make up the majority of what was to become the 99th Pursuit Squadron and later the 332nd -- the famous "Tuskegee Airmen."

When Sherman and I applied for the Civilian Pilot Training Program, you could see all the propaganda preparing the country for war. There were ads and posters with the Uncle Sam pointing and saying, "The army wants you. Become an aviation cadet and get $245.00 a month." On top of that you would get combat pay and other hazardous duty pay. All tolled it would come to be about $400.00 dollars a month. That was a fortune in 1941. A private in the Army got $25.00 a month. Sherman and I wanted in on that. Only, we knew we couldn't. The Army was segregated and there were no black fliers.

Then on January 16th 1941, Congress authorized the formation of an all black fighter squadron to be trained in Tuskegee, Alabama. I knew right then that was what I wanted to do. I obviously liked the idea of being an officer a lot more than being an enlisted man. Sherman and I talked about all that money and the adventure of being a fighter pilot. We knew it wouldn't be easy. The struggle wouldn't be with studying or learning to fly, however; the struggle would be the fight against discrimination. In 1941 there were no black officers in the Air Corps. But that was about to change because thirty-three were to be trained as the first black aviators. I wanted one of those thirty-three slots and so did Sherman. But first we needed to learn to fly.

Sherman and I were accepted without question to the Civilian Aviation Program and took the flight lessons at the University of Chicago. It was in two parts. First, we had our primary training. That entailed getting our private pilot's license and learning to fly Piper Cubs. It was a lot of fun and relatively easy compared to studying for my major. Although we were only being taught basics, the only part of flying that was even challenging was landing. A lot of the guys had problems with landing but our instructor was so good, and he explained it so well, that even that was easy. When landing, a lot of guys tried to slow down on their way in. They would throttle down too soon and end up dropping a dozen feet only to bounce hard on the tarmac. Our instructor explained that you flew your plane right off that tarmac, inches off the ground. You were flying no different than if you were a thousand feet in the air, only you were just inches off the ground. Then, you would throttle down enough to stall. The plane only had inches to drop. You ended up skimming along the runway, making a perfect landing – no bounce.

When we finished primary training in 1940, we went into advanced training -- the second part of the program. Advanced taught us to fly Waco's, and that was invaluable because the military used Waco's to train their new pilots. It was immediately obvious that the Civilian Aviation Program would give a huge advantage to any student (who took it) over a normal cadet who hadn't taken it. It would be like taking the same course twice.

Our instructor was Jack "Buff" Woolams, a graduate of MIT (Massachusetts Institute of Technology). He was an Army test pilot. If he hadn't been killed in a test flight years later, Chuck Yeager might never have been so famous because Woolams was originally designated to fly that record speed flight. Anyway, he taught us well and we had a lot of fun learning to fly. The first thing he had done was to make us drive a car, to test our coordination. I remember it because Sherman had never driven a car and didn't know how. Somehow he managed to stay in the class. Sherman took to flying like a duck to water.

After I graduated from the program, I looked forward to becoming one of the first black pilot officers in the United States Army Air Corps. I just had to get accepted. Since I already had my private pilot's license and had been flying for months in the very plane the army was using to teach its new pilots, I figured I'd be a shoo-in. All I needed was to take the army flight exam.

I went to the post office in Chicago and took the test. It was hard! Especially on the eyes. There were seven of us that tested that day. I was the only black man. I knew I was physically fit and I had good eyesight. That was the key, good eyesight. You had to have 20/20 vision. I tested 20/10 in one eye and 20/15 in the other. Anyway, I was the only one who passed that day. The other six all flunked it. So now all I had to do was wait. I knew they'd take me. I had taken the Civilian Aviation Program; I'd passed the army flight exam; I had my private pilot's license; I'd been flying for over a year in Waco's, the very plane the army trained its new cadet pilots in, and I had a letter of recommendation from Buff Woolams. How could they not take me? Why would they opt for someone with no flight experience over a candidate with extensive training? Well, they did!

I sat waiting and waiting for word to arrive that I'd been accepted, but the weeks turned into months and all the while I read in the papers how the military was screaming for pilots and the battle of Britain was raging and everyone knew we were going to be at war soon. I watched with growing anger how the government was teaching hundreds and hundreds of white pilots, with no flight experience at all, to fly a plane that I was already proficient in. Why were they not taking me? I had good grades, in a tough major, from one of the better colleges in the country. I was already a good pilot and I was ready. I had good letters of recommendation from my instructors. I wanted to go! How could they not take me? Well, they just didn't. I waited half a year for that telegram and it never came. Finally I realized that if I didn't do something about it myself, I was never going to get in. So I sat down and wrote a letter to the First Lady of the United States, Eleanor Roosevelt. [ii] It read:

Dear Mrs. Roosevelt.

I am a student at the University of Chicago. I have applied for acceptance as an Aviation Cadet in the Army Air Corps. I have passed the physical examination and have waited several months to be called up for duty. I am a graduate of the Civilian Pilot Training Program at the University of Chicago and have received my private pilot's license.

I am aware of the program to start the first Negro flying school with the 99th Pursuit Squadron. I had hoped to be accepted into that program. I would be very grateful for any assistance you might be able to give me to help me attain my goal.

Yours truly,

Clarence C. Jamison.

After I signed it, I mailed it off. I didn't think Mrs. Roosevelt would even receive the letter, but within three weeks I received orders to report to the Army Air Corps so I knew she must have turned it over to someone.

I was so excited! I told everyone. My mom and dad, Phyllis, my uncle, everyone. I knew they were all proud of me. I would be among the first black Americans to become a pilot and an officer in the United States Army. At first, my parents were elated, but they immediately became fearful. I was to report to Tuskegee, in Alabama. In the south.

TUSKEGEE ALABAMA, AUGUST 1941

My parents warned me! "Don't you go down there," they said. They knew the perils! In the black community, it was just understood. People disappeared in the South. That's the polite way they talked about lynching and murder. I hadn't been south of Akron, Ohio, since we had moved from Arkansas when I was five. My family occasionally traveled to Chicago to see my uncle, but that was west, not south.

Blacks had to be careful in the south. That was just the way it was. Still, it was quite a shock for a northern black man such as myself to enter a world of segregation, to see signs over drinking fountains and bathrooms that said, "Whites only" or "Colored," to not be able to walk into a restaurant to eat because it was for "Whites only."

When people read about discrimination like that, which was normal in the 1930's and 1940's, they get shocked and enraged. Was I enraged? No! Who was I to be enraged about the segregation in the south and at Tuskegee? I expected it! I knew that just because the Army Air Corps accepted me, nothing was going to change down in Alabama where there were still lynching blacks. I wasn't going to let anger and hatred eat me up. But I knew I had to be careful. There were certain things that were an immediate death sentence. Like getting out of line with a white woman. And I don't mean dating her. I mean, say something to her; or not getting off the sidewalk for her; or not giving up your seat for her. It was horrible! Future generations have no idea how bad it was, just like I have no idea about the hell my great grandparents went through before the Civil War and after, during the reconstruction.

When I first reported to Tuskegee as an aviation cadet, there wasn't even a base yet, just the Tuskegee Institute campus. There were 12 men in my class and I was very pleasantly surprised to find out that one of them was from Cleveland and I knew him. It was the little brother of my grade school friend, Bill Brooks. I had not seen Sidney Brooks for years. Sidney had grown into a stocky kid, much bigger and sturdier than I was. Sidney had gone to Ohio State. Now we were together in Class 42-D. We were the second training class. The first class of 12 was well into their training.

We were billeted in a long open hall with double bunk beds in the bathhouse on campus. [iii] The campus provided us with room and board. We were aviation cadets, and as the first black Americans to become future pilots in the U.S. Army Air Corps, we were treated like kings. We even had good food. The woman in charge of the mess hall was real nice. Her name was Mrs. Drew. She was a kind, attractive, gracious woman and we all liked her. She was married and though probably only fifteen years older than the rest of us, she treated us like we were her kids.

There were twelve of us, but we dropped to eleven fast. One night, before we had even started flying, I was sound asleep when I woke to rushing movement. One of our guys went flying past me to run full speed into the wall. He knocked himself incoherent and the other eleven of us were wondering what the hell made him run into the wall like that. It turned out that he had epilepsy. He was discharged because of a physical condition. Because the country was not yet at war, he didn't have to stay in the armed forces and was discharged to go back home. I felt bad for him, but it was probably a good thing. He might have killed himself. He was the first guy in our class to wash-out.

We started our training in August of 1941. Alabama was hot and humid. I never got used to that heat. I knew I would never make my home in the south, not only because of the racism, but because of the climate: it was too hot and too humid.

I was commissioned into the army as an aviation cadet. Because we were going to be officers in the United States Army, they really put it to us during training. It was very rigid, the typical stuff you see in movies about basic training or boot camp. "Forward march! Right shoulder arms!" and all that stuff. We marched often and took turns leading each other.

25

As Army officers, we had to learn all aspects of infantry training. We had to take apart, clean, and put back together all standard infantry weapons. Then we took them to the firing range. We fired Springfield .03s, Browning Automatic Rifles, Tommy Guns, pistols, and shotguns. The shotguns were used for skeet shooting and they were our first introduction to hitting moving targets, a kind of prelude to aerial fighting. We had to achieve a certain degree of proficiency, just a minimum of success at things like marching and weaponry.

We had a lot of PT (Physical training). There was daily running and calisthenics and we did one ten mile hike with full pack. At the same time that we had marching and weapons instruction, we continued our other classes. Our learning was intense. We had aerodynamics, meteorology, ground school, military justice, learning articles of war, Morse code and many other classes. We had to be able to understand and punch out Morse code quickly. We did it all. We had some pretty sharp guys. We also had a wide range between the colleges, too. I came from the University of Chicago, which, in 1941, was up there with Harvard. James Wiley was a graduate of the University of Pittsburg and Bill Campbell (both Wiley and Campbell were in a later class) had attended the Tuskegee Institute where Booker T. Washington was a teacher. Being from Cleveland, Brooks went to Ohio State. Dryden went to City College of New York. We had some smart guys. We could all handle the scholastic part. It was the flying part that washed guys out.

Even with all those classes, we were aviation cadets first. We were at Tuskegee to learn to fly. I soon completed my primary training in PT – 17 (Primary Trainer) aircraft. These were open cockpit, two-seat biplanes. Our training was excellent.

At Tuskegee we had both black and white instructors. They were real good. Our basic flying instructors were black. There names were Charlie Foxx and Milton Crenshaw. Charlie Foxx taught me basic and he was one of the best pilots I have ever seen. He was an acrobatic pilot. I remember one time when we were training in the PT-17, the open cockpit, dual seater, and Charlie decided to show me something. We had been practicing precision flying and had gone through slow rolls, snap rolls and loops-- all that kind of stuff. One day, while we were practicing, just goofing off really, Charlie says, "Cadet Jamison, I want to show you something." With that, he flipped us over so that we are flying upside down and he purposely stalled the aircraft...while we're upside down! I suddenly find myself inverted, terrified, and spinning down! The centrifugal force was trying to hurl me out of my seatbelt and my legs were flopping around. My hands are holding on for dear life and I was almost ready to panic when Charlie snaps the controls. Boom! The plane righted itself and we were flying steady and

27

straight again. I was still charged with adrenaline and I said, "Charlie, what the hell is going on and what was that?" He said, "That's a Dilly! I named it that." Now it's called an inverted snap roll. Years later, after the war, I was talking to some gals that were stunt flyers at the air races and they'd heard of the "Dilly."

Charlie taught me the Dilly because it was very important to learn how to recover from a stall. Stalling is exceedingly dangerous! The only time anyone ever *wants* to stall is when they come in for a landing, literally inches off the ground. Higher than that means you'll be dead. Now, the instructors deliberately make you stall and we practiced recovering in all types of aircraft. Anyway, when my instructor did his snap roll, flying upside down like he was, we were slowing down. By trying to maintain altitude, he was losing airspeed. Once the plane reached the critical point when it could no longer fly, it stalled and flipped over. Then it dropped! That's when Charlie did the snap roll. It was violent!

But the thing they drill into your mind, whenever you stall, is to dive. It's almost against a person's nature to push that stick down and head for planet earth, but that's what you have to do. Your first impulse is to pull back, but if you do, you'll fall like a leaf from a tree. So you force yourself to push it down. This is the only way to control the plane and recover from a stall. You force that nose down and pick up your airspeed. You

28

use your ailerons to stop the rotation and when you finally get enough speed back, you pull out of the dive. It's very important not to pull out of a dive too early. If you don't have enough airspeed, you will stall again, only now you won't have the altitude to recover. I've seen guys get killed because they pulled out of a dive too abruptly. A pilot has to remember that his plane is twice as heavy during a dive because of centrifugal force and additional G's. The increased weight will make a plane stall much faster than it normally would. I've watched pilot's stall at ten thousand feet and recover nicely, only to pull out too early, before they have the necessary airspeed. They immediately stall again only now they are at five thousand feet. Now they don't have the needed clearance between themselves and the ground to enable them to regain airspeed. Anytime you go straight into the ground, whatever the terminal velocity, you'll die. It's like going into a concrete wall at one hundred miles per hour. I saw a lot of men die because of stalls, especially after the war when I became an accident-investigating officer.

Of course, some planes are trickier than others, like the P-39 Aerocobra, where the engine was in the middle of the plane and not in the nose like most other aircraft. That made it easier for the plane to get into a dangerous flat spin and harder to dive once stalled. To compound matters, because of that flat spin, if you tried to bail out, the propellers could cut you in half as you tried to parachute to safety. I didn't much care for the P-39.

Our training was both extensive and intense. After basic with Charlie Fox, I went into primary where we started training in the BT- 13's (Basic Trainer.) These were enclosed cockpit planes with non-retractable landing gear. I learned quickly just how good my civilian instructor had been and how well he had taught me. He didn't just teach me to fly. He also taught me the physics behind flying. If I did a slow roll, he made me learn the forces acting on those ailerons and things like that so that I knew what would happen before I felt it from doing it physically in my plane. It is just so important to have that kind of training. The thing that killed so many guys was the stalling out. You had to keep your airspeed up.

We were assigned different instructors to take us through the different phases. In primary we had several white instructors. They were good pilots. Captain Robert Rowland was one of my instructors. He was a good man. He loved to fly and was a genuinely good guy. He wanted to see us succeed and helped us develop as pilots.

Captain Robert "Mama" Long was another and he was also a great instructor. He didn't have a racist bone in his body. He agonized if he had to wash someone out. That was why we called him "Mama." I was glad when Brooks was assigned to him. Of course everyone wanted Rowland or Long to teach them. I never flew with Mama Long. There were several other instructors, including Captain Clay Albright and Lieutenant Colonel Noel Parrish, our base commanding officer, who occasionally took men up. All our white instructors were real good pilots. All but one was a human being. That was Captain Robert Lowenberg.

Lowenberg was a racist. He was the polar opposite of Mama Long. Lowenberg was a good flyer, but he was quite simply a poor excuse for a human being. It's interesting, that in the future, with all the combat I was to see and all the contact with white pilots, I was never to see any racism at the front among combat veterans. It's the rear echelon officers like Lowenberg in the safety of the caste system back home who made their own war and fought it back stateside against their fellow countrymen. Lowenberg was an officer, but he was not a gentleman. He did a lot of little chicken-shit things to try to demean us. Needless to say, those of us who got Lowenberg as our instructor now had two things to worry about: our demanding training regimen and the frowning, dis-approving eye of an instructor who held a preconceived notion that we were incapable simply because we were black.

Because of our many brushes with men like Lowenberg, nationwide, the black community had very little trust in the ubiquitous white leadership and authority. There were very few white people willing to stand up to the injustices and bigotry.

31

But Eleanor Roosevelt was one who did. While we were training in Tuskegee, she came down and toured our base. Charles A. "Chief" Anderson took her up and flew her around. [iv]A lot of people know nothing about Chief Anderson. He was a great man, a great teacher, and a true pioneer in aviation. He died in the 1990's at age 90. He did a lot of flying and most of it was self-taught. Even after I rotated back from Europe with all my flight and combat experience, he still could have flown circles around me. The day Eleanor Roosevelt asked to be taken up and flown around, the Secret Service tried to talk her out of it. "Nonsense!" she said. She was going up. The Secret Service even called the president to try to stop her. They said, "The First Lady wants to fly with these black fliers down here." The president simply said, "You know Eleanor! She is going to do what she wants to do!" She was a strong-willed woman. She flew around Tuskegee in a little Piper Cub, the safest aircraft we had, and put Tuskegee on the map in the eyes of the American public. She was a remarkable woman. Eleanor was a hero in the black community. When she flew with Chief Anderson, we thought, "Wow, we have Eleanor in our corner."

That wasn't the first time Eleanor had done something to recognize the contribution of American blacks. Marion Anderson was a famous black singer. Her voice was magnificent. But the Daughters of the American Revolution wouldn't let her sing at Constitutional Hall. Why? Because she was black! That was the kind of stuff that was going on and had been going on for years and years. And that's nothing. That was high profile discrimination. The everyday injustices done to the common black man, woman and child were one hundred times worse. Anyway, that was one reason American blacks loved the First Lady. Eleanor resigned from the D.A.R. because they wouldn't let Marion Anderson sing. The black community trusted Eleanor. She was one of the few white Americans who stood up to injustices.

Despite our distrust toward white leadership and authority, we were fortunate to have such a good commanding officer in charge of the Tuskegee Army Airfield training school, Lieutenant Colonel Noel Parrish. Parrish was a good man. He was a hell of a pilot. He gave me a check ride in the PT-17 and had me doing figure eights and other maneuvers. He said helpful things like, "Make sure if the wind is blowing that you are crabbing just right." I was good at it and he was happy with my performance. Parrish was a smooth pilot. Being "smooth" back in the '40's is like the term "bad" today, meaning he was good.

Our training continued! We trained sun up to sun down and besides our constant flying; we were in the classroom learning about navigation, weather, the mechanical functions of our planes and everything pertaining to flight instruction.

There wasn't a lot to do outside of training. We were usually busy studying but we played cards once in a while and occasionally we saw USO type shows, performed by black entertainers. Lena Horne came to Tuskegee once and Joe Louis came down and put on an exhibition fight with one of our PR officers. They made a big deal about it and the PR officer got in the ring. Apparently, he'd done some boxing before. The first round started and they danced around. This officer comes out and throws some punches at Joe, who blocked them all and kept moving around. The PR guy starts thinking he's pretty good and is fairly aggressive. After a few minutes of this shadow boxing, Joe steps back, salutes, and then pops this guy right in the mouth. The officer almost went down, but Joe was just toying with him. He kept dancing around. Joe never tried to hit him again after that. Joe was probably just letting him know not to get too cocky, or else. Joe could've killed him.

Our training went on and it was intense. The attrition rate was high. Every young black pilot lived in fear that his dreams would come crashing down around him and I don't mean in an airplane either. We all wanted to succeed so badly and knew that if it didn't happen, we would never get another shot. If a white pilot washed out of fighter training, he could still be a pilot. He could go on to fly less demanding aircraft like transports or bombers. He could keep his dignity and stay on as an officer with a future and an income. If a black pilot washed out, he was out! No second chance to fly any other aircraft! No job! No income! Since we were at war, all he could expect was be transferred into the Army to serve as a cook or some other non-combat detail as a private getting $25.00 a month.

Some of the guys who washed out of my class and the classes after me would have made great aviators, too. They'd have been an asset to the Army Air Corps. And there was a tremendous need for pilots. The military needed pilots to ferry planes to Europe and the Pacific, to carry supplies all over the world and to fly bombers, recon planes and transports; you name it. The country could have used those black pilots. That is one reason the idea of segregation was so wrong and so stupid! It was such a waste of manpower. It was the same with female pilots, too, but that's just the way it was back then.

Out of our original twelve, four washed-out before we hit our sixth month. I already knew how to fly and I even found the training difficult. That was why I marveled at guys like Brooks. Unlike me, Brooks hadn't gone through the Civilian Aviation Program. He had no prior flight experience and he was learning from scratch, and still passing. To me that was damn impressive. Although I hadn't known Brooks very well before training, once we became cadets together, we were best of friends. I helped him and tried to look out for him as much as I could. But he didn't need much help. He was good!

Our training progressed and other classes followed behind us. It's interesting to note how many of us were from Cleveland. Of the twenty-eight pilots who made up the original 99th Pursuit Squadron, four of us were from the same town. Benjamin O. Davis, who was in the first class, was from Cleveland. He had lived just down the street from me. Brooks and I, from the second class, were from Cleveland and Irwin Lawrence, who was in the class after us, was too.

Autumn passed and soon it was December of 1941. I had just completed primary training and was half way to being commissioned as one of the first black officer pilots in the U.S. Army Air Corps. I was very excited because I'd received extended leave to go home for Christmas. I went to Chicago first to get Phyllis and then together we took the train to Cleveland to see my parents. Phyllis and I weren't engaged to be married yet but that was only because I didn't have enough money to buy a ring. We had an understanding, though. We were going to get married when I graduated from Tuskegee and was commissioned a lieutenant in the Army. If all went well, that would be in April. Only six months away! We arrived in Cleveland around the first of December and I was halfway through my two-week leave when my mom called us in to the living room. Something I'd never heard in her voice made me hurry. It was around 1 pm and we all listened to the radio in stunned silence.

36

Aviation Cadet Clarence Jamieson climbing into an AT-6 trainer at Tuskegee, Autumn of 1941.

At Tuskegee, climbing into an AT-6 advanced trainer.

WAR

The date was December 7th, 1941 and the Japanese had just attacked Pearl Harbor. As we gathered around the radio, not one minute had passed when my mother turned to me with a worried look on her face and said, "Don't you have to go back to camp?" I laughed, "No, mom, I'm just a cadet. They can't use me. There's nothing I can do." We listened to the descriptions of the devastation and mounting casualties all afternoon before hearing President Roosevelt's address. I went to bed that night knowing that soon I would be smack dab in the middle of World War II. But that was a while off. I had to finish my training. And I still had a week's leave and I was determined to make the best of it. Well, just to show how parents always know more than their children, the next morning I get a telegram: "Report back to camp."

When I got back to Tuskegee, most of us wondered if the higher-ups were going to try to speed up our training to get us into the war. Germany had just declared war on the United States and the news from the Pacific was all bad. The Philippines and Wake Island were besieged; Guam had fallen; the British fortress in Singapore had surrendered. We were terribly outnumbered in the air, land, and sea and needed every last pilot that could fly a plane. But you didn't rush flight training. That was how men died. Our training class stayed on its normal schedule. We had a high enough attrition rate as it was. Out of the first class of twelve, only five made it. They were Lemuel Custis, Benjamin O. Davis, Charles Debow, George "Spanky" Roberts and Mac Ross. Out of the second class of twelve, my class, four had already washed out, leaving eight and our training wasn't finished.

When I was almost through primary and my training was going well, or so I thought, Lowenburg would not pass me into advanced training. Lowenberg said I lacked the aptitude. If I couldn't pass to advanced, I'd wash out. Major Rowland, however, knew I was a good pilot and didn't understand what the problem could be. He decided to take me up to see for himself if what Lowenberg had told him was true. Much to my surprise he took me up for a test in an AT-6. I'd never even been in an advanced trainer, only the BT-13, a basic trainer. The AT-6 was a far superior aircraft. Major Rolland had more confidence in me than Lowenberg ever did and he wasted no time.

We took off, climbed, and almost immediately he did a full roll. Then he said, "Okay, Cadet Jamison, you do it." I did it beautifully. Then he did a barrel roll and told me to also do it. Again, I did it perfectly. We went through the whole routine. Barrel rolls, loops, and so on. By the time we finished, he was pleased. "I don't see any problem," he said to me. To the great chagrin of Lowenberg, I was immediately passed into advanced training in the AT-6 aircraft.

The AT-6 was a closed cockpit plane with retractable landing gear. It had a radial engine. It was the equivalent of the P-36 fighter that the Army used before the war. We weren't to see a plane with an in-line engine, an Allison and Rolls Royce, until we flew the P-40, which was much more streamlined, giving it a much greater speed. A radial engine is a round, air cooled engine, whereas, an in-line engine is more streamlined and is water-cooled.

In the next few months, four of our remaining eight washed out. That meant of the original twelve, there were only four of us left – me and Brooks, Charles Dryden of New York City and James Smith of Cincinnati, Ohio. Toward the middle of March we began to breath a little easier, knowing we could see the light at the end of the tunnel. We knew we still had to be careful, however. We could still wash out for screwing up legitimately, and there was Lowenberg.

A few more weeks passed and we were almost through advanced. Then, on a Navigational flight, James Smith messed up on his cross-country direction and got lost. It might have been because Lowenburg was flying with us. You had to be extra careful because he'd look for things to try to get you on. I can't imagine having done it myself, but we are all human and flying with Lowenberg didn't give anyone confidence. We've all done some dumb things but Smitty messed up and Lowenberg washed him out with less than two weeks to go. He had completed more than seven and a half of his eight-months training when they got rid of him.

Other than Smitty, I believe *some* of the others were legitimately washed out because they didn't have the aptitude to fly *fighter* aircraft. One or two might have killed themselves. But regardless, only three of us graduated and that was wrong. Those five other pilots who washed out were good pilots. Smitty was a good pilot. If he'd been white, he would've either made it or gone on to fly bombers or transports. Because he was black, he was kicked out. Some of the white pilots who passed through Kelly and Randolph weren't as good as the men who washed out of Tuskegee. Our commander, however, wanted the best of the best. Because we were the vanguard, the pioneers of black America in combat aviation, he wanted only the absolute elite to represent Tuskegee. With the intense spotlight he knew would be on us, he needed and demanded the best.

Some of our guys thought there was a quota and that was why so many men got kicked out, but I didn't feel that way. I know that did happen, too many times, but for the most part, I really think they wanted the best flyers --or you were gone.

By now, Brooks, Dryden and I were feeling pretty good. We could see the light at the end of the tunnel. But with one week to go, the three of us committed a minor infraction and

Lowenburg put us on KP for it. I don't even remember what it was and we were probably wrong, but none of the other white instructors were after us the way Lowenberg always was. He was always trying to degrade us. There we were, aviation cadets, days away from becoming officers in the United States Army Air Corps and he put us on KP in the mess hall. To this day I've never heard of aviation cadets pulling KP, either before or after us. It was demeaning. We were scrubbing pots and pans and doing whatever the cooks told us to do. All the other cadets were laughing at us. It really wasn't that big a deal, but, it's not something that should have happened to an aviation cadet. Lowenberg delighted in it. To add insult to injury, he came in the mess hall to check on us, to make sure we were being properly abased. At that point, Mrs. Drew came in for something. Beautiful, kindly, nice Mrs. Drew, the woman in charge of the mess hall. Lowenberg saw her and said in his blunt, rude, degrading way, "Hey, Drew, you need to ..." We didn't even hear the rest. His tone was just so derogatory. He didn't call her, "Mrs. Drew." He just spat "Drew." To us that was the worst form of disrespect! It was intolerable! It wasn't deliberate, that was just Lowenberg's constant attitude toward blacks because he was a spoiled punk with the unfortunate rank of captain. He knew how much we all liked Mrs. Drew and his tone and lack of respect was a slap across the face. That was it! We didn't care if they washed us out or not. It didn't matter at that point if we got kicked out. You can only take so much. He had insulted a nice, lovely, kind, black woman. I equated her to be like my mother. All three of us were outraged and bolted up towards Lowenberg but Brooks beat both Dryden and I to him. He marched right up into Lowenberg's face.

"Captain Lowenberg, I don't appreciate you addressing that woman without using her deserved title "Mrs." Drew." The words he used were respectful, but the tone of his voice, the speed of his speech, the look on his face, and his body language was extremely aggressive. That's what he said, but the literal translation was, "Your ass is beaten if you don't back up right now!" Lowenberg was well over six feet and big, but Brooks was a solid guy too, and we all had a chip on our shoulder about racial stuff. With a seething Brooks in his face, Lowenburg turned purple. He didn't dare do anything and knew he'd crossed the line. He knew he was wrong. Furious, he turned around and stalked out without saying a word. It wasn't any kind of victory, though. It was just sad. You couldn't get through to someone like Lowenberg.

Then the day we'd waited for finally arrived -- graduation. It was the day Lowenberg got his revenge. Our ceremony was scheduled for 10:00, but since Lowenberg still had not relieved us of our KP duty, Brooks, Dryden and I reported to the mess hall early that morning. At about 8:00 we received word that Lowenberg had moved our graduation ceremony to 9:00 and we now had one hour to prepare. We had no way to inform anyone of the change in time. The ceremony was held at 9:00 so everyone missed it by one hour. The only witness to the graduation of class 42-D was Mrs. Drew, who heard about it and quickly hurried over.

Nonetheless, graduation was quite a feeling. Only three of us had made it -- Sidney Brooks, Charles Dryden and me. Out of the first class, 42-C, five had graduated, so with them, we now totaled eight black pilots flying in the U.S. Army Air Corps. I was one of them. We were the first pilots to make up what was to be the 99th Pursuit squadron and eventually become the flight leaders and commanders of the famous Tuskegee Airmen.

Left to right. Clarence Jamison, Charles W. Dryden, Sydney Brooks and James Smith. Smith was washed out one week before graduation. More than seven and a half months through our eight-month training.

The 99th Pursuit Squadron

Phyllis was still in Chicago. I missed her very much. That says a lot too because in Tuskegee, we were it! We had the money, we were officers, we had the prestige and the cool uniforms and we flew fighter planes. All the girls wanted the pilots. But the day after I graduated flying school, I planned to go up to Ohio and marry her. I was to be commissioned a second lieutenant on April 29th and on April 30th I was to be married. When I graduated, I wanted to leave immediately for Chicago to marry Phyllis, but I didn't have any money. I had two hundred dollars coming, but payday wasn't for five days. I had leave orders but no cash. That was a problem! My pass was only for two weeks. I'd waste half of it before I could afford to go.

I had a friend named Jack Rogers, who'd been a Kappa Alpha Psi fraternity brother of mine back at the University of Chicago. Jack was now at Tuskegee, too, only he was still a cadet. I asked Jack if I could borrow the money. Jack didn't even blink. He just got the money and handed it over as if I was borrowing a pencil or something. Of course, I paid him the minute I got back, but it meant a lot to me. Jack and I are still close, even to this day. To show you the type of guy Jack is, a few years later I brought it up and thanked him but he didn't even remember it.

I departed on my two-week leave after graduation and left for Chicago where Phyllis and I were married. My mother threw us a reception in Cleveland and after that my wife and I drove to Tuskegee because I had to report back.

My friend Sidney Brooks had also gotten leave and returned to Cleveland. By this time Brooks was like my little brother. Because he had had no formal training before Tuskegee, I always tried to help him. As a result, we'd grown close. He married one of my best friends from grade school and high school, Lucille Miller. They drove back down to Tuskegee with us. That was a neat time in my life, driving down to Tuskegee with my wife beside me, my friends with us, and my future ahead of me.

Once I graduated and was commissioned an officer, I no longer had to stay at the Tuskegee Institute. I was able to find my own billet and my wife and I began to look for a place to live. My wife and I were invited to live with the principal of the local black high school. He had a very nice home. At the time, Tuskegee was completely segregated. We had a movie theater, a school, a store and other shops typical of every small town in America so there was no need for us to go out of the segregated areas. We had everything we needed right there in Tuskegee. Also, you didn't give some southern whites the opportunity to mess with you. It was bad for any black person in the south, but for Army Air Corps officer cadets, it was especially bad because during a time of war, we could be tried for mutiny.

Here is an example of the everyday harassment a typical black American might encounter. One of the only times my wife went out of Tuskegee was when she and Lucille took a bus to Montgomery to go shopping. They were leaving a store when an old white sheriff stopped them. "What youah girls doin' and what-cha got in them bags?" Then he nosed his way into their belongings and shopping bags. My wife was appalled. She'd grown up in Cincinnati – the north – and she'd been raised in a well-to-do family. They didn't dare protest the sheriffs search. I guess he was looking to see if they were smuggling booze or something. Anyway, he let them go, but my wife was angry when she got home. "He certainly didn't address us as ladies," she said. Here were two well-dressed young women out shopping and minding their own business and they get harassed. It wasn't right, but that's just the way it was in the South. Imagine the outrage if a black man had done anything remotely similar to a white woman. That was why we never left the base or went into "white" Tuskegee.

Phyllis and I had a normal life on base. We went to the exchange for everything we needed. We went to the military chapel on Sundays. We went to the officers club to socialize and to the many dances. They had a theater for us so we saw all the latest movies. That was how I got my nickname, "Jamie Boy".

There was a pirate movie called, "Black Swan" starring Tyrone Powers as the swashbuckling hero "Jamie Boy". Tyrone Powers was one of my favorite actors. There were a rare few black actors but not any with leading roll parts, only supporting roles. All a black actor could hope for was a part as a supporting role, like in "Gone with the wind", another great movie. We watched all these movies and the irony of the times was not lost on us, but that was just the way it was and there was nothing we could do about it. Like in Casablanca; here you have a middle aged black man, "Sam" being called a boy by the leading lady who was obviously twenty years younger than him. You have two best friends, Sam and Rick, yet the white man calls his friend "Sam" while the black man calls his friend "Mister Richard", even though everyone else in the whole movie calls him Rick. Did we mind it? Yes, but what could we do about it. Actually, we were happy that a black man could get such a wonderful part in such a famous movie. The song, "As time goes by" is an all time great that will last throughout the ages. We thought it was a great that a black person was even given the opportunity. That was just how blacks were portrayed. It was degrading. We were human beings deserving of respect. But what could we do? White society had to grow up and accept us as human beings and that took time. Blacks gradually received more dignified roles.

By the time we graduated, we were extremely confident. Of course we were "shave tails" (brand new lieutenants) but we were well-trained pilots. Our thorough training was to save our lives many times over in the coming years. We had P-39's for a while but they were already considered obsolete. Finally, we got the P-40's. That was a nice plane and it was easily recognizable to people because the Flying Tigers had made it famous fighting in China. We never had teeth drawn on our aircraft, but they were the same plane. We didn't have anything to compare it to at the time except for the P-39's and other training planes so we thought it was the greatest. It wasn't until we went into combat and ran up against the Focke Wolf 190's and ME-109 German fighters that we realized we were outclassed. The P-40 wasn't a great dog-fighting plane, though we did it with success, but it was a great strafing plane. It could endure a terrific amount of punishment. I was to find that out firsthand from the enemy in the next few years. It was like flying a tank. It was also mechanically reliable except for one time, which would be instrumental in my development as a pilot.

We often made navigational flights as part of our continued training. I was on a roundtrip flight from Tuskegee to a base in Georgia when I had some engine trouble. I was forced to land at the Atlanta Municipal airport. They had a group of civilian mechanics there, all white guys, and they gassed me up and looked at my engine. I told them, "Check the magnetos. She isn't running right." I walked over to get a Coke and just milled around while they worked on my aircraft. Now a fighter plane in a civilian airport during a time of war was in itself kind of exciting. A lot of people started showing up. Apparently, word had spread pretty quick that a P-40 had landed at the municipal airport and people came to look at it. It was a formidable-looking plane. Add to that, here I stroll out, a black man in southern Georgia in 1942 wearing my head covering, goggles and jump suit. I can still see the stunned shock registering on all the faces. I can even overhear things like, "There is a black guy getting ready to get in that fighter plane!" and "The pilots a Negro!" Several hundred sightseers are now lined up. After I climbed in my plane and taxied out to the end of the runway, I called time and got ready to take off, but I notice that one of the twin mags still wasn't working right. It was running rough. My first instinct was to go back in and have the mechanics fix the bad magneto or to have Army mechanics flown in from the closest military air base to fix it. I knew that although these Atlanta guys might be great mechanics, they weren't used to working on military aircraft. But I saw hundreds of people - all white people – and all watching to see this fighter plane take off. There wasn't a lot of military flight traffic in this area so the curiosity was enormous. There was a real interest in flying in those days, too, because it was still so new. Add to that, the latest and most famous U.S. plane, a P-40, piloted by a black man. I had really drawn quite a crowd.

Well, that one mag didn't look too good and I knew I should go back to the hanger, but there were so many people watching, white people, and I knew if I went back the entire crowd would be disappointed. Half of them would probably be saying, "What do you expect with a black pilot? He's chicken shit!" So I talked myself into trying to make it back to Tuskegee where they could fix it properly. I started down the runway and I got to about 90 mph when the mag started popping like mad and the needle began bouncing all over the place. My engine was coughing and sputtering and blowing black smoke. I was really having trouble, but by then I was committed. The runway was rushing up on me and all I could see was a wall of trees ahead. I took off and barely cleared them. The tower called, "P-40! YOU ARE CLEAR TO LAND, ANY RUNWAY!" They knew as well as I did that I was in big trouble. I got to about two hundred feet and started losing power rapidly. I made a real gradual turn so as not to lose air speed and came back around. I just barely made the runway, put my wheels down, and landed. I tell you, I was never so glad to be back on the ground as I was right then. I taxied back to the hanger where the mechanics were waiting for me and I knew I was going to be there overnight. There was too much work that needed to be done on my plane and the civilian guys didn't have the experience. I called

Tuskegee and they said they'd send some mechanics over to fix it the following day.

Since Atlanta was segregated, arrangements were made for me to I stay with a black family. They were very hospitable. That night as I lay in bed, I thought about what had happened. I thought about how stupid I'd been. That's how people got killed. I knew that plane wasn't right! I should have taxied back to the hanger, but there were so many people watching, white people, and I knew they'd think I was afraid. They'd say that a white pilot would've been able to take off, and, what do expect from a black pilot? I was so worried about the expectations of these white people that I almost got myself killed. I was too damn proud. Right then, I thought, that from that moment on, I wasn't going to let my ego get my ass killed. I had nothing to prove! I was a hell of a good fighter pilot! I'm sure I wasn't the only one who did something dumb like that, but that was the pressure of being in a unique situation as a black man, in those times, in that part of the country. That was the defining moment in my training, and maybe my life. It was absolutely invaluable in my development as a pilot and as a man.

Since the Army Air Corps was segregated and we didn't have enough pilots to form a unit, we simply trained while the classes behind us came through, adding more pilots to our pitifully small numbers. We trained and trained and got better and better, but it was boring. We read about the war and were itching to do our part and prove ourselves. While brand new white pilots were being shipped off immediately to war, we stayed at Tuskegee and trained. Since we were so bored, we looked for anything to break the monotony.

Once, when I was out on training flight at a few thousand feet, I saw a matronly black woman in a field putting out her laundry. She reminded me of my mother. Mom always did laundry on Mondays. I got a devilish impulse and maneuvered around so I could come at her from behind. I poured on the coals and dove and all the while she was completely unsuspecting. I got right over her head at only two hundred feet going 350 mph. She must have thought the world was coming to an end. She threw her hands in the air and it looked like she was having a heart attack. Her laundry went flying and the prop blast blew it all over the yard. I thought it was funny for about a second. Then I felt terrible. Poor woman, here it was a beautiful, sunny day and this fighter plane came sneaking up on her to scare her to death. Not only that, her clean laundry was all over the yard. I felt so bad about it I never did anything like that ever again. I also never told a soul about my first dubious strafing run until 2002 when this book was being written.

We trained constantly and at the end of the sessions, we'd break off into dogfights. Dryden and I were fooling around once, dog-fighting, and we ended up coming head to head. Dryden says there were four of us, but I only remember it

55

being the two of us. I think if there had been four of us, someone would be dead. Anyway, Dryden and I are coming at each other at over 300 mph. It wasn't like we were playing chicken. We both tried to get out of the way to get into a position to maneuver around behind the other, but twice we both went the same way, like two people on the sidewalk stepping into each accidentally as they both try to move aside for the other. We literally had seconds before impact. Somehow we managed to maneuver just enough to miss each other. As I recall, I went up and he went under and it scared the hell out of both of us. The very next day after our training session, however, we were back dog-fighting.

On a separate navigational flight, I was flying my P-40 to New Orleans, Louisiana and back. I landed at the municipal airport to gas up for the flight back. It was the same scenario as when I had landed in Atlanta some months before -- an Army War-hawk fighter plane landing at a civilian airport flown by a black pilot. A huge crowd grew as they refueled my plane and I hopped out in my jumpsuit and strolled over for a Coke. Every eye in the airport was watching me. Of course, they were almost all white people. As I was getting my Coke, I notice this older black man watching me. He was a custodian at the airport, wearing his worker's overalls. Suddenly he said to me, "You one a them flyers from Tuskegee?" The black community knew all about us (So did the whites) but Tuskegee was in Alabama.

Everyone at the New Orleans Municipal Airport was wondering what I was doing in Louisiana. I say, "Yeah, I'm from Tuskegee." He just nodded but then he said, "You know, a few weeks ago there was a British guy in here with a Spitfire." [v] I said, "Oh yeah." I wasn't sure what he was getting at. Very nonchalantly he adds, "When this British guy left, he did a little show for us." He waved his hand side to side to show me how the plane had dipped its wings back and forth. That was all he said. But it dawned on me that what he really meant was, when you leave, what the hell are you going to do? By this time there are literally hundreds of people standing around, watching. I had an audience.

I walked leisurely back to my plane, hopped in and taxied out, routinely. I took off, gained altitude, and got my airspeed up. Then I called back to the tower. "This is Army Air Corps number whatever, permission to salute the field?" The tower says, "P-40, you are clear." I turn back toward the airfield, low, and come screaming in at full throttle. I was right above the runway and I'm going over three hundred miles per hour. My plane was moving and I was really making some noise. Just before I got to the airfield, I pulled up and did a slow roll right off the deck. I hit the apex of my roll directly over the airport. I looked down at the crowd, finished the roll and screamed out of sight on my way back to Tuskegee. I just knew for sure that my ol' boy down there was raising his fist proudly, saying, "Go, boy!"

Our training continued. We were steadily growing in numbers as Jack's class graduated behind us, but we still didn't have enough for a squadron. My friend from the University of Chicago, Sherman White, was with us now and we were a small, close-knit group. We got along extremely well although we cuffed at each other like lions. Especially in the air! To keep a bunch of hotshot pilots like us in order required a good military man. That man was our commanding officer, Lieutenant Colonel Benjamin O. Davis. Davis was all military! He was the first black man to attend the United States Army College at West Point. As a cadet, he was given the silent treatment. Not one other cadet talked to him his plebe year. That gives you an idea of the kind of mental toughness he possessed. Before he became an aviation cadet, he had already been a professional soldier for years, so he was perfectly slated for command of the 99th Pursuit Squadron. Since he'd been interested in the Army Air Corps – the squadron was a perfect match for him. We were just a bunch of civilians who had finished our cadet training and were commissioned as second lieutenants. We needed to be trained as officers in the United States Army Air Corps. Who better than a West Point man.

Benjamin O. Davis was aloof. He wasn't too approachable, except on business related matters. He wasn't going to get buddy-buddy with a peon. I was just a junior officer, a lieutenant, so he wasn't going to talk to me even though we knew each other from back home in Cleveland. He lived just down the street from me growing up. Davis was sharp and he was good. He had to be! They had tried hard to kick him out at West Point and failed. Davis had to be three times as good as a white cadet. You have to give the man his due. Davis commanded the 99th Pursuit Squadron and later the 332nd, the only fighter squadron never to lose a bomber under its protection. He led some of those raids over Berlin. By then he was a general and he earned those stars. [vi]

The thing about being a fighter pilot was that crazy things and dangerous stunts were almost expected of us. Like that time in New Orleans. Here I was, doing a slow roll at one hundred feet over hundreds of civilians. I could have been court-martialed for that. You had to be a little wild to be a fighter pilot. Though we weren't immune to punishment for our behavior, we typically were given a lot more leeway than other officers.

While we were waiting to get shipped overseas, the rumors spread like wildfire. There was a lot of debate as to where we would go. The Pacific? Europe? China/Burma/India,

59

where the Flying Tigers had made a name for themselves? We were all itching to do our part but, I couldn't complain. I had it pretty good. My wife lived in Tuskegee and I was able to go home every night. Also, there were black USO shows that came to the base and performed down at the hanger.

One night a real big name came to perform at our base. I think it was Count Basse, though it might have been Jimmy Lundsford, I can't remember whom. Anyway, everyone was there to see him. Everyone! It was that big. It was holiday time for the other military personnel, but we flyers had to keep training. We had our schedules and our flying had to go on. That afternoon we were in our P-40's practicing dog fighting-- Sidney Brooks, Spann Watson and me. I could see the huge crowd down at the hanger, watching the show, and I guess the devil made me do it because I said over the radio to Spann and Sidney, "Hey, I'm going to give them a show." We came in on a normal approach although we were coming in fast and I asked the tower for landing instructions. They gave us the okay and we came down that runway in a staggered formation. I was first, then Brooks, and then Spann. We were really moving and all this is right in front of the USO show. I'm sure Count Basse stopped whatever he was doing to watch us because we were that close. And that loud! I come down right off the deck, pulled up and did a slow roll out of the landing pattern. I turned it over and let my wheels down while I was upside down. Then

I finished the roll and landed. We never planned to do this but Brooks saw me and mimicked me exactly. Spann, not to be outdone, does it. The USO show was only two hundred feet off the runway and everyone saw us and, boy, was it cool. We were all laughing in our cockpits and it was fun!

But as we taxied in, who is waiting for us in his staff car? Davis. He was pissed off! We got out of our planes and walked over to him. I got to him first because I had parked first. He says to me, "Okay, Jamison. You looked good, but you are grounded for a week." Brooks and Spann got the same punishment. That meant we were restricted to base, which meant I was in trouble with a much higher authority than Davis -- my wife! She was furious. She'd been home cooking me dinner when I phoned her. Because of that stunt, I couldn't come home for a week. She was mad!

We did crazy stuff because we were so frustrated. We are reading about the Desert Fox (Rommel) raising hell in Africa and the battle for Guadalcanal is touch-and-go yet we weren't allowed to fight. Colonel Davis understood our frustration. He couldn't show it, but I think he was proud of our spirit.

One thing about our time at Tuskegee, we had fun. We had some real personalities. Dryden, Brooks, and I were close, but we quickly made friends with the other guys graduating in the classes behind us. Lee Rayford was one of them. He was good enough to do stand up comedy, he was that funny. He'd sit down in the mess hall pretending to be flying his fighter. He'd make gestures like he was manipulating a joy stick, all the while poking at fake instruments and pretending to be talking on the radio. He'd answer himself by mimicking controllers or other guys. The entire mess hall would be roaring with laughter. Rayford told jokes all the time and they were hilarious, but the one I remember in particular was when he gave advice about what to do in a dogfight. "If you've got a Jerry (German) on your tail, and you can't shake him," he said with a dead serious look on his face, "take off your seatbelt and run around the cockpit screaming "Help! Help!"

Sherman White, my buddy from the University of Chicago, was a great pilot but he never looked the part. When people think of a fighter pilot, they think of a dashing, striking figure, like Erwin Lawrence, Bill Campbell and some of the other guys. Sherman was laid back and easy-going and his uniform was always a little disheveled. We constantly had to remind him to straighten up. Nat King Cole's song, "Straighten up and fly right" was a hit song back in 1942 and became a catch phrase for us at Tuskegee. We said it to Sherman a lot.

Bill Campbell was an athlete. He was a great tennis player and a hell of a pilot, one of the best we had. Campbell was tall and looked the part of a fighter pilot. He was a southern boy and a real nice guy with a great sense of humor.

Charlie Hall was a quiet guy and a hell of a flier. He was short like me but real stocky and built. He was also a good athlete. The funniest thing about Charlie was in the evening when we would have a BS session, drinking beer. Everyone would be clowning around and when Charlie had a little bit to drink, he'd start singing, "the signifying monkey." It was a real long song and just went on and on but Charlie knew every verse. It was about a monkey that gets into trouble. It was real dirty but funny as hell. The guys would try to get Charlie to drink just so he would sing it.

We had some real good guys and some great pilots. As soon as our slowly growing ranks swelled to where we could muster twelve pilots, they asked us to do a fly-over of the airport. We took off with twelve P-40's in four flights of three planes each, all in V formation. They wanted to film us from the ground and they had movie cameras set up and ready. I lead our flight of three and we were the last flight. I was flying with Bill Campbell and Charlie Hall and we all knew we had a hot trio.

The camera crews filmed each flight as it passed over and then it was our turn. I said to Bill and Charlie, "Our flight's going to be better than these previous ones." They were both great pilots, and glancing to my sides, I saw we were looking good, in a tight formation. We had permission to fly low and went across the field in a tight V. As we passed behind the other flights, the air was unexpectedly turbulent. We were bouncing

63

in this tight formation. As I came across I looked again and Bill Campbell had tucked his wing between my tail and wing, literally inches from my fuselage. He was so close it took me by surprise. He was too close. I quickly turned back to the front and the next thing I knew, my plane was jolted. My nose popped up so hard the stick was ripped from my hands. Bill's wingtip bumped my rudder. It was partially my fault because I hadn't anticipated the prop blast from the previous flights, the last of which had passed seconds before. Campbell's wing tip hit the rudder of my tail but luckily his wing came under my rudder, not over it. I had had a good grip on the stick but he hit me so hard it broke my grip. I said, "Oh shit!" It was so totally unexpected and violent! My nose shot straight up and I grabbed for the stick. The motion was so violent that the mud on the cockpit floor shot up into my face. I grabbed the stick and pulled down, forcing my plane to level off again. I didn't have my goggles on and now I had big chunks of dirt and mud in my eyes but I knew I had to keep my eyes open. My vision was blurred and my eyes were burning like hell and watering. Bill knew he'd hit me and saw me work to get control of my plane. "Hey? You okay Hoss?" We all called each other Hoss. I said, "Check out my tail, what's my damage?" Bill says, "It's okay. It's torn but you should be okay."

I don't know if they got that on film or not. A lot of guys were surprised when I landed and pulled in with a ripped elevator from the collision. We asked the mechanics and other ground personnel if they'd seen anything but nobody knew we had had a mid air collision. It was a pure fluke. We were both at fault -- me for not anticipating the turbulence/prop blast and Bill for being a little too close. But like me, Bill wanted to make it look good and we knew we were three of the hot pilots. Bill felt terrible about it but it could have been much worse. If he'd hit my elevator downward, I would have crashed. We were too low and I wouldn't have had the time to pull up.

We had a bunch of hotshot pilots. We were confident and we were good. All we did was train. They wouldn't let us fight, even though we had hundreds of hours of experience. While other pilots graduated and were sent off to join combat units with the bare minimum of required flying hours, we kept training. The Army couldn't figure out what they wanted to do with us, for over a year. All the combat groups wanted a wing. A wing consists of three squadrons, a total of 72 planes. We could only form a squadron if every black pilot in the United States Army Air Corps was included. That's a total of 24 pilots. What would they do with us? Where could they send us? As a result, we continued to train.

Besides my friends who were good fliers like Brooks, Jack and Sherman, some of the others were James Wiley, Spann Watson, Charlie Hall and Bill Campbell. Charlie was a flight leaders so that tells you how good he was. Spann Watson was in my flight. Spann was also good flier, very steady, very reliable. So was Jack Rogers. Sometimes we would practice acrobatics in formation. I remember Jack kept having problems doing the loop in the P-40. He could do it just fine in our trainers, but the P-40 was a heavier, trickier plane. In the fighter Jack would stall and fall. He could always get out of the spin and regain himself, but he was frustrated. Finally, we went up together one day and I said, "Get on my wing. It's not hard. You have to fly the plane through the loop. As you start pulling up and become upside down, don't put too much pressure on your stick. Fly with the same amount of G's you had flying straight and level. It will carry you through the loop. If you don't fly through the loop, you'll stall." Jack was a good wingman; he would get right in there and stay there, three or four feet away. Close! The closer you are, the easier it is because you immediately see any change. You won't notice it if you are twenty feet away, at least not in time. I began by doing lazy eights. Just a big gentle barrel roll really. Then I started making the barrel rolls bigger and bigger and soon we were doing loops. He is right with me, four feet away, in tight formation. Then I hear over the radio, "Hey, I'm doing the loop." He didn't even know he was doing it because he was concentrating on staying with me. He was a quick learner anyway and never had any trouble again.

James Wiley, an engineering graduate from the University of Pittsburgh, was a very good pilot too. I used to measure the guys in dogfights to see how I could do against them and I was never able to beat Wiley. I could never get on his tail. I could beat most of the other guys but Wiley was the toughest I ever went up against in a dogfight. But he never got on my tail, either. Charlie Hall and I were evenly matched, too. I could never beat Charlie but he couldn't get me either. I don't ever remember anyone being good enough to get on my tail. We would start at 12,000 feet and come at each other head first as 400 mph. After the pass, we would maneuver and circle and fight for positioning. I did everything I could think of to try to get Charlie, but I couldn't. We'd be doing loops and circles, and one time I did a snap roll at the top of my loop to try to get him. He was below me and I hoped to come out of it in position to get him. It didn't work. He did something to counter it. It was a dangerous maneuver and unexpected, but we ended up in a tight circle, losing altitude. I could usually get most of the other guys when I did the snap roll on top of the loop, but I couldn't get Charlie. We had to break off our dogfight because it was getting too dangerous. We were getting too low. It was just understood that when we broke it off, it was a tie.

There were usually eight of us practicing. At the end of the day, after we'd finished maneuvers, when we saw each other, we would get into formation and head for home. Sometimes, though, without a word, we would just attack each other and break into dogfights. We had some really hot pilots but in my opinion, Bill Campbell, Charlie Hall and James Wiley were the best. Bill Campbell could always take everything I could throw at him too. Davis knew about our flying ability so he made Charlie and me flight leaders.

I remember one time after we had been training, Brooks and I had just flown in and Erwin Lawrence was standing there with a photographer. The photographer was from Cleveland and he wanted to take a picture of the Cleveland pilots. It was kind of extraordinary that so many of us were from Cleveland. Davis wasn't present, although he too was from Cleveland, but the photographer snapped a photo of Brooks, Erwin, and me. [That is the photo on the cover of this book.] It was a great picture and I'm glad he took it. Little did I know, that picture of our training days at Tuskegee would be one of my cherished photo's later in life.

In April, 1943, we finally received our orders. The 99th Pursuit Squadron was shipping off to war. We left Tuskegee on a troop train to New York's Camp Shanks, our embarkation point. We had no idea where we were going but there was much speculation between England, the Pacific and North Africa? On our way from Tuskegee to New York, we passed my brother Thurston's unit. He was an officer with the 366th Infantry.

Thurston was also slated to go overseas, but he didn't know where. I didn't have time to see him, though, we passed straight through to Camp Shanks where the entire squadron was together, prepared to ship out. We pilots were the high profile members of the 99th, but there were hundreds of other black servicemen that were part of the 99th that had been trained, just as we had, for their duties. Because of segregation, we had to be able to operate as an individual entity so we had our own ordnance, our own mechanics, ground crews, cooks, quartermasters, MPs, and every other type of servicemen required to keep a fighter squadron operational. On April 15, we boarded a transport ship, the USS *Mariposa* and pushed out into the Atlantic.

It was my father's ultimate joy to see me become something. When I became
a pilot, my dad came down to Tuskegee. I could see the pride on his face. It
was one of the best feelings I've ever had. My father never even owned a car
and there was his son taking off in a fighter plane.
--Front row. Herbert Carter, Lee Rayford, George "Spanky" Roberts,
Benjamin O. Davis Jr., Lemuel Custis, Clarence Jamison, Charles Hall.
--Second row, Walter Lawson, Spann Watson, Allen Lane, Paul Mitchell,
Leon Roberts, John Rogers, Louis Purnell, James Wiley, Graham Smith.
--Third row, Willie Ashley, Charles Dryden, Irwin Lawrence, William
Campbell, Willie Fuller, Richard Davis, Sidney Brooks, Sherman White,
George Bolling.

The P-40 Warhawk.

NORTH AFRICA

Standing on the deck of the *Mariposa* besides Sidney Brooks, Sherman White, and Erwin Lawrence, I watched the eastern seaboard get farther and farther away as we headed out into the Atlantic Ocean. It was shortly after we pushed to sea that we found out our destination. We were going to North Africa. I couldn't know it at the time, but of the four of us, I would be the only one to return from the war alive.

We crossed the Atlantic heading for French Morocco. There were four hundred members of the 99th Pursuit Squadron aboard the *Mariposa*. There were also 3,500 white troops aboard ship, heading overseas to Africa. Colonel Davis was in command of all troops aboard ship.

Wary of U-boats, we made it across without incident and arrived at Casablanca on April 24. We moved to Oued N'ja, near the town of Fez, where we received our aircraft. Our planes were beautiful! We'd never flown brand new planes before and mine even had "Jamie Boy" written on the side. The names of everyone's planes had already been picked out. Dryden flew "A train" (he was from the Bronx) and Sid Brook's plane was "El Cid".

Casablanca was interesting but not at all like Hollywood portrayed it. Casablanca and Fez were part of French North Africa so all the locals spoke French. We went to the Kasbah and enjoyed ourselves. It was especially fun for me because I spoke French. Everyone always wanted to go out with me. The famous singer/actress, Josephine Baker, had lived in France most of her life but she fled to French Morocco when the Germans invaded. She was there when we arrived. Josephine invited Colonel Davis and some of the guys to see the sights with her.

After a few weeks there, I received the first of many V-mails I was to get from my wife. I found out I had a daughter; Michal Jamison, born April 25th, the day after we arrived in Casablanca. My daughter was the first girl born in the squadron. "Spanky" Roberts had a son but I think my daughter was born before his son.

From Casablanca we flew across North Africa, making several stops before reaching Tunis. The flight was beautiful. For us, it was brand new territory and the Atlas Mountains to the south and the blue Mediterranean to the north was magnificent to see. At one of our stops, Colonel Philip "Flip" Cochran, a combat vet, was there. He got the nickname "Flip" from the well-known comic strip character "Flip" Corkin from "Terry and the Pirates." He flew with us and taught us tactics. Cochran was a regular guy and a great pilot.

We started flying immediately, going up with Colonel Cochran and practicing aerial tactics. Flying P-40's, we knew we weren't going to do much high altitude fighter escort. The P-40 wasn't good for that. It was a low level fighter and since Flip Cochran was a dive-bomber pilot that was how we started.

When we arrived in Tunis, the war in Africa was already over. Rommel had been driven off the continent, although the squadron we were assigned to had a heyday shooting down German transports trying to evacuate the remains of the Africa Korps to Sicily. But from our base in Tunis, the war in the Mediterranean was officially on for us.

The 99th was commanded by Colonel Davis with Spanky Roberts as his Operations Officer. Erwin Lawrence was Assistant Operations Officer. The three flight leaders were Lemuel Custis, with A flight, myself with B flight, and Charlie Hall with C Flight.

When Davis made me a flight leader, I began to lobby to get guys I wanted in my flight, like Brooks, Dryden and Rogers, among others. Each flight leader wanted the best pilots and I knew all of them could fly. Brooks and Dryden were in my class at Tuskegee so I knew them well. Jack Rogers had been in my fraternity at the University of Chicago so I knew him too; he also was a good pilot. I asked for them and Davis okayed it. B Flight consisted of myself, Brooks, Dryden, Rogers, Lee Rayford, Leon Roberts, Willie Ashley and Spann Watson.

74

Literally within days of arriving at our base, I had my first close call. I was leading my flight, B Flight, on a routine practice run. In North Africa, the ground is low and flat. We did a number of different exercises, including low level flying. When I say low level, I mean, just above the ground. We were hauling ass over the North African plains at 250 mph less than twenty feet off the ground. Suddenly I saw these high tension electrical wires. I didn't have time to yell or do anything except pull up. I just made it, the wire whipping past. My wingman, Leon Roberts, was beside me, just a little behind. He had the same split second to react. He went under the wire. The other planes went over the wire and then we were all back together again. Within seconds Roberts called me on the radio and said, "I hit something." I closed in and looked at his aircraft. The wire had hit the top of his tail and sliced it right off: sheered it off like someone used a giant razor blade on it. He had just barely avoided decapitation. How Leon Roberts was still able to fly, after colliding with a high tension wire, I don't know, but he made it back to base and was able to land. The incident scared the hell out of me!

We were initially attached to the 33rd Fighter Squadron. Because we didn't have enough pilots to form a squadron, we were assigned to a white fighter wing. The 99th Pursuit Squadron was on one side of the airfield and the 33rd fighter squadron was on the other. Although we were separated by a few thousand yards, we held our briefings together. On June 2, 1943, I flew my first combat mission. It was against the German/Italian-held island of Pantalleria, between Africa and Sicily, west of Malta. Pantelleria was strategically important because it lay between Africa and Sicily. Before the invasions of Sicily and Italy could begin, the island had to be neutralized. It had coastal batteries, 88mm anti-aircraft guns, an airport and underground hangers to protect and field at least 80 aircraft. Its steep cliffs and coastal defenses along with dangerous currents discouraged amphibious assault. Pantelleria would have to be bombed into submission before any assault in earnest would begin.

There were four of us ordered to a briefing at the other end of our airbase. Bill Campbell, Charlie Hall, James Wiley and I were chosen because we were the hot pilots. Only Wiley wasn't a flight leader. I was a captain by then and a flight leader, but not for this first mission. We were each assigned to a flight; seven white pilots with one black pilot. This was our first introduction to integration. I was assigned as the wingman to a white fella who was only a lieutenant but he'd seen combat before. He said, "When we take off, just get on my wing and stick with me." We were going on a dive-bombing mission. The formation had two groups of four making up the eight-plane flight, all in pairs with the flight leader and his wingman in front, then another plane and his wingman.

We were flying on our mission and getting close to the island when I noticed these strange-looking black clouds. Then it dawned on me. These weren't clouds. It was flak. "Damn! They are shooting at me!" I got angry. I thought, "What the hell are you shooting at me for?" Of course, I was ignoring the fact that I had a damn five-hundred pound bomb underneath my belly and six .50 caliber machineguns, and I was getting ready to go down and bomb and strafe them. But that is the reality of war.

The radio crackles and I hear the lieutenant I was flying with say, "Stick with me." He didn't go into any detail. I guess what he thought was that I would follow him down and strafe and bomb after him, but we were used to doing it in formation (and we had practiced and practiced) and were just so cool about it in the 99th Pursuit Squadron. He pealed off and went into his dive and I stayed right on his wing. He glanced over and was so surprised that he did a double take. He didn't expect me to be right on his wing in formation, but I wasn't going to let a rookie lieutenant leave me behind. He smiled and in we went. We strafed and dropped our bombs and we were much more effective than if we had gone in separately. It was a successful mission and we blew the hell out of little Pantalleria. We flew back, landed, rearmed, and went back again. We bombed and strafed that little island twice that day and when we left, it was burning with black smoke trailing into the air.

Our logbook showed that I had three flights that day, the two missions to Pantalleria and a ten-minute flight. Since we were on one side of the airfield and the 33rd was on the other, about a thousand yards away, we had to go down to their end for our briefings. The ten-minute flight was because bomb craters surrounded the airfield. This airfield had been German before we took it and it had been bombed relentlessly before the Axis retreat. When the allies took it over, they filled in the craters on the runway but not along the sides. With planes taking off all the time, we couldn't taxi down the middle of the runway. Bill Campbell went to taxi to his briefing on one of our first days. A pilot can't see well as the nose of the plane is high when it's on the ground. Bill accidentally taxied into a bomb crater. You can just imagine how embarrassed he was. We all had out little goof-ups, but we razzed him unmercifully for that. Bill had to get his plane jacked out of that huge hole and after that we all just took off, circled, and landed on the far side of the airfield. There was just too much debris and too many craters everywhere else.

I wondered how I would do when I actually saw combat for the first time. You know, you have these self-doubts. Everyone does. It's kind of like when you are playing football or something. You wonder how you're going to do when the chips are really down. But we had confidence, too. We knew we were well-trained. I had over 300 hours in the P-40. I figured I had more experience in the P-40 than some of the combat veteran white pilots we flew with. We had been training in Tuskegee for over a year. That was a lot of experience. Our training was exactly the same as that of the white pilots at Kelly and Randolph field.

We were a bastard unit attached to a white wing. No one knew what to do with us and no one wanted us. They all wanted a wing but it takes 3 squadrons to form a wing. We were only there to satisfy the politicians, so they could say, "We've got some black flyers over there!" We were only there to fill a quota. It didn't mean a thing. But we never encountered any racial discrimination with the white pilots at the briefing. There was camaraderie amongst pilots, especially among combat veterans. Black, white, red, yellow, we could care less about policy. The white pilots were fine. Some of their commanders hated us, though. It was the rear echelon and some of the higher ranking, non-combat white officers who hated us and wanted us discredited.

There had to be a beginning, though, and that's the way integration of the U.S. military started. Some reporter dubbed us, the "Lonely Eagles," but that was a PR name. We never called ourselves that. I don't buy into that image and I never thought of us like that, although there sure weren't many of us. An organizational chart gives an idea of how few of us there were. A wing needs 3 squadrons. A squadron needs 3 flights.

A flight is 8 planes. Our entire squadron only had 24 pilots. As more black pilots were trained -- and we had guys graduating from Tuskegee every 5 weeks -- we would eventually have enough pilots to form the 332-fighter wing, to which we were attached. Later still, the 477th bomber group, was formed.

On June 7, 1943, I led my first mission, five days after our attack on Pantelleria. We were returning to bomb and strafe the little island again and since I had been there a few days before, I was chosen to lead it. After that first mission, I was told, "Ok, you're on your own." We made another dive-bombing run and it was very simple. We would repeat what we'd done a few days before. We would get there in about 30 minutes and the main challenge was to recognize the targets. We had been well-briefed with recent aerial photographs and our target was a supply depot. We had 12 planes on that raid and we dove down and dropped all twelve five-hundred pound bombs on that depot. We received flak, but we didn't encounter any German planes. Our mission was successful and we returned to base. After flying combat missions and then leading my own flight, I started gaining confidence. It's one thing to believe you can do something, but there's nothing like actual experience to cement your confidence.

We continued with our missions. On June 9, a number of our planes from the 99th Pursuit Squadron were on bomber escort duty for twelve Douglas A-20 Havoc attack bombers

80

when four German ME-109 fighters appeared. There was no action. The enemy planes --superior to our aircraft-- simply climbed, got above the P-40s, and got away. I was flying that day, but I wasn't on that mission. I heard about it from Dryden, though. He was one of the pilots on that mission. That was the first indication that our planes weren't as good as our enemies. The German fighters could outrun and out-climb us.

On June 10, Dryden and Lee Rayford were on bomber escort duty with two P-40s from another squadron and some British Spitfires when they were attacked by ten ME-109 and Focke-Wulf 190s. The P-40s stayed with the bombers while the Spitfires drove off the German planes. Another learning experience; the Spitfire, like the 109s and 190s, was superior to our P-40s.

On June 11, British troops landed unopposed on Pantelleria and then it was on to Sicily. In July of 1943, over 3,300 ships assembled in the Mediterranean in what is still today the largest fleet ever assembled in world history. [vii] The 99th Pursuit squadron helped support the invasion and all through July we flew combat patrols and low level strafing and bombing missions for both British and American ground forces.

We didn't see any German fighters for almost two months. Then on June 18, six of our P-40s encountered four Me 109's near Pantellaria. Sidney Brooks was one of the pilots and he was the first to spot the German fighters. The 109's were above them and dove. In the ensuing dogfight, Lee Rayford's P-40 was damaged. He got behind two 109s when a third got on his tail. The 99th damaged three German aircraft before the 109s broke off, one trailing smoke.

This kind of action continued, but the enemy always broke and ran. In our slower planes, there was no hope of chasing them. If we were to engage, it was up to the Germans. We were only fast enough to stay in the fight. Besides, we had escort duty and couldn't leave the bombers. I was flying missions almost every day and although there was always anti-aircraft fire, I never saw any German fighters.

On June 21, members of the 99th were on bomber escort when they encountered German fighters approaching. The P-40s broke off from the bombers and dove on the attackers. The Germans broke and ran. There were no casualties.

Our bomber escort missions continued, mostly to Sicily, but for over a month we never encountered any German fighters. Then, on July 2, on another escort mission, some of our guys ran into a whole batch of Focke Wolfe 190s and ME-109s all at once. There were almost fifty German planes. Charlie Hall damaged a 109 and shot a Focke Wolfe out of the sky and became the first black U.S.A.A.C. pilot to shoot down an enemy fighter in the Second World War. I was flying that day, but I was a flight leader on a different mission. The 99th shot one down and had two probables. Charlie was a good friend of mine and when I got back, he told me about it. He was pretty excited. German fighters, two Me-109s, were on Charlie's flight leader's tail. Charlie intercepted them. As he was telling me his story, he broke out laughing. "I was aiming at the first guy," referring to the German flight leader, "but I hit the second guy." The wingman!

Sadly, with the good news came some very bad news. Two of our fighters still hadn't come back. We kept waiting for them to appear in the distance, but they never did. One of them was my friend, Sherman White; the other Charles McCallum. They were both listed as missing in action. We never knew what happened. There were rumors and it was said that they'd had a midair collision, but we never knew for sure. I took Sherman's loss hard. I had known him since we were freshmen at the University of Chicago. We had taken the Civilian Pilot Training Program together. He and Brooks were my closest friends. Our entire unit took the loss of Sherman and Charles McCallum very hard.

The press made a big deal about Charlie Hall's victory. We were getting a lot of press anyway, as the first black squadron to see combat, a lot of attention. It was nice, too, because it meant some people were happy that we had done something good for the war effort. There was one reporter in particular who had promised a coca-cola for the first black pilot to make a confirmed kill on an enemy aircraft. This reporter brought a coke all the way across the Atlantic and North Africa. We also had several black war correspondents who would send stories back to the black newspapers. There were national ones like the Chicago Defender, the Pittsburgh Courier and the one down in Norfolk, Virginia called the Afro-American. A picture of Charlie holding up that coke was pasted on newspapers across America.

General Dwight D. Eisenhower was in the area and he even came to congratulate Charlie for his victory. The military turned it into a real big deal. The entire squadron was there, except for a few guys on patrol. Eisenhower flew in with the British Air Marshall and a bunch of brass. All the big wigs! They had a formation on the flight line where Eisenhower congratulated Charlie and they gave him a medal. The Supreme Commander came in his own plane with his own mechanics and visiting entourage. I was curious about the plane because I'd never seen one like it and thought, "What the hell kind of damn plane is this?" I walked over to check it out. I saw this short man in a flight suit, whom I took to be a mechanic, hanging around near the plane, kind of off from Eisenhower's entourage, so I walk over to him. We started to shoot the breeze for a few minutes when someone walked over to him very stiffly and said, "General Doolittle…" I don't even know what else the guy said, my jaw just kind of dropped when I heard the name. I thought, "Uh-oh, I better straighten up." This wasn't a mechanic or a sergeant. I had been talking to General Jimmy Doolittle, the famous pilot who had flown the bomber mission against Tokyo off an aircraft carrier. He didn't wear any rank insignia's and just seemed so casual compared to the rest of the brass. I'd had no idea who he was, but that was the kind of man he was. He didn't want the attention that so many other generals reveled in. Here was a general, talking casually with a lieutenant. I said, "Sir, I saw you fly in the Cleveland air races." We talked about that for a few minutes. He flew a little GB speedster and I used to go out to Hopkins airfield and sit on the runway to watch the planes roar by. It was a big thing in Cleveland. What a coincidence that we would meet on an airfield in North Africa. Whatever interest I had in flying started there. That air show was one of the reasons I became a pilot. Jimmy Doolittle was impressive. There I was, in my 20's, and he was a lot older than me, and he had flown a bomber off an aircraft carrier. Something I couldn't imagine doing. Years later I would barely remember meeting Eisenhower and shaking his hand, but I clearly remember meeting and talking with Jimmy Doolittle, as if it were yesterday.

After Eisenhower's brief visit, it was back to the war. Most of my missions were dive-bombing missions, but sometimes we flew fighter support for bombers. An interesting fact about our unit, on bomber support missions, our commander, Colonel Davis, made us fly the entire mission with the bombers. Right in there with them on their bombing runs, right into all that flak! Davis led some of those missions himself. We were probably the only fighter squadron in the service that did that. I don't know how practical it was as no German fighters went in there, either, because of all that flak, but we did it anyway because it helped us stay with our bombers for the return home. We would weave back and forth, always above them. Being above and looking down is a natural position to be in for escorting fighters. If we were below the B-25s, we wouldn't be able to keep our speed up if we had to climb to protect them. The reason we would weave back and forth was that we didn't dare slow down to our bomber's speed or we would be sitting ducks if enemy fighters appeared. We wouldn't be able to engage them while they dove on our bombers.

At this time, some of the missions we supported were British. They had twin engine Baltimore Bombers. I'll never forget an incident that I watched from the ground. We were at our base in North Africa when a British Baltimore Bomber came in for an emergency landing at our airfield. The bomber had gotten into trouble and was shot up pretty bad. They were in bad shape, down to one engine, and were really struggling. On the way in the pilot overshot the runway and I don't know what he was thinking, but he tried slowing up. Maybe he thought he could still make the field, but he would have been better off just keeping his speed up and landing in the desert. We were standing there watching him come in and he was at about six hundred feet when he stalled. He dropped straight down. Like a rock. That big ol twin-engine bomber went right into the ground. Crash. There were no survivors. There was nothing left! If that pilot had just kept flying and made a controlled landing in the desert, even with flying speed, he and his crew were a thousand times more likely to have survived. I remember thinking to myself that I wouldn't make a good bomber pilot. They were just too slow. Even with all that firepower they carried with them they were just big targets in the sky.

On July 3, twelve of our P-40s were on bomber escort with forty-four P-40s from another squadron. They were protecting twenty A-20 and A-30 bombers when they were attacked by five German Me 109s and Fw 190s. The enemy aircraft made one pass and rolled away. There was no damage done by either side until the allied aircraft made their bombing runs. There two of the A-20s were shot down. Later that same day, two of our guys got probables against a pair of Fw-190s.

On July 4, eleven P-40s from the 99th and twenty-four P-40s from another squadron were on bomber escort when they encountered two Fw-190s. The enemy fighters were quickly driven off. A second mission encountered three Fw-190s. Again, because of our sheer numbers, the enemy aircraft were forced to flee.

On July 11, twelve of our P-40s encountered twelve Fw-190s attempting to attack allied ships making the landing at Licata, Sicily. The P-40s drove off the enemy fighters without loss to either side, but Lieutenant George Bollings P-40 was hit by German antiaircraft fire. Bolling was forced to bail out and floated in a dingy in the Mediterranean until air sea rescue came and got him.

All this time we were flying out of our base in North Africa. Make no mistake, there is nothing romantic about war, especially in the North African desert. The climate is appalling. In the summer it is unbearably hot; worse than an Alabama summer. The billets were uncomfortable. Everyone was lonely for his family. We were isolated in the middle of the desert with nothing around us for miles, bored out of our minds. There was nothing to do.

We were bored but we found things to do. Somehow, Brooks and I got a hold of a case of .45 caliber ammunition for our sidearm's. We always talked about what we'd do if we were shot down. The thought of surrendering to the Nazi's was not pleasant so we decided we'd better practice. Firing at empty bottles and ration cans, we got pretty good. We fired that whole case and it was just me and Brooks doing the shooting.

James Wiley was an intellectual; a quiet, studious type. He was an engineer before he'd become a pilot. While we all tried to salvage destroyed German motorcycles and vehicles for our own use, Wiley found a wrecked Focke Wulf 190 that was still in decent condition. He and his mechanics repaired it and Wiley flew it around the base. It would have been nice for all of us to learn to fly the enemy plane just so we could know its capabilities and limitations, but the danger of being shot down by our own anti-aircraft and fighters from different squadrons was too great.

To alleviate boredom, we played poker for hours on end. One of my treasured memories in North Africa was playing poker with Colonel Davis. He wouldn't play poker with just anyone. I was only a flight leader, but one night I ended up in a game with him. Everyone wanted to beat him because he had rank. We wanted that field grade money. Also, he was good and he hated to lose. At anything! Anyway, we were playing stud poker and I had already lost a few times that night, but in the first round of the next hand I took one look at my card and raised the pot. Just a little, but it was enough to get some of the guys in the room to say, "Uh-oh, Jamie's got something!" Now that was precisely what I'd hoped for because I didn't have a damn thing. I was bluffing. But I had planted the seed and everyone thought I had a hole card. The second hand was dealt and I promptly raised again. Once more there were comments from people around the table, "Watch out for C.J." Then the third hand was dealt and it was face up. I drew a four. I raised a little and then when the fourth hand was dealt. I got lucky and drew another four. One of the guys drew a pair of queens and I raised him in the face of his pair of queens with only my two fours. Everybody was saying, "Ohhhhh, Jamie's got a locks!" meaning I had a good hand. They thought I had two pairs when I really only had one. Davis was watching quietly, but he'd been betting, too, so he must have had something good. Then I raised the pot by a few dollars and everyone dropped out but him. Davis was thinking it over and watching me. I stared back at him, my eyes giving away nothing. Suddenly, he threw his cards down. Now, nobody likes to be bluffed out of a winning hand. Davis was a hell of a good poker player and he hated to lose. Hated it! He folded the winning hand and I'm sure he didn't appreciate it when I showed my hole card of nothing. I'd beaten everyone with a pair of fours. The room exploded with laughter, except for Davis. He looked like he was going to have me court-martialed.

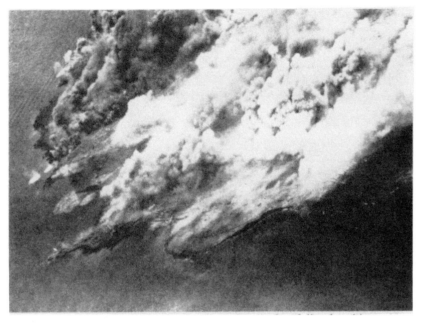

The Island of Pantelleria seen from the air after weeks of dive-bombing raids.

Me in front of "Jamie Boy" in North Africa

Members of Flight "B" sitting, left to right, 2nd Lt. Leon C. Roberts, 2nd Lt. John "Jack" Rogers. Squatting, 2nd Lt. Spann Watson, 1st Lt. Charles Dryden. Standing, 2nd Lieutenant Willie Ashley Jr., 1st Lt. Lee Rayford, 1st Lt. Clarence Jamison and 1st Lt. Sidney Brooks. (Photo by Thomas W. Young, U.S. War Correspondent.)

SICILY, August 43

The 99th Pursuit Squadron was assigned to the 33rd Fighter Group and was moved to Licata on the southern coast of Sicily on July 28, 1943. We flew close air support and dive-bombing missions out of Tunis in support of Patton's troops and Montgomery's British troops as they took Palermo and Messina. Our dive-bombing missions were almost always against gun emplacements or pillboxes. Intelligence would give us pictures of the targets at our briefings along with navigational instructions on how to get there. I hadn't seen any enemy aircraft, but we took a lot of ground fire. Some of the guys came back with shot up planes. I remember coming back from one mission and I thought the operation had been a piece of cake. Then I saw one of my guys had a big hole through his tail. Luckily, the shell didn't explode and just punched a hole through his plane. But it made me realize how things were a little more precarious than I had thought.

We continued our missions, but there was almost a complete lack of enemy air activity to contest the skies. But that didn't mean it was easy. The Germans had excellent anti-aircraft crews. That was because they had so much practice.

I was leading B flight on another mission and we were flying over an agricultural area with squares of farmland below when I noticed four flashes, one coming from each corner of a particular square field. Maybe a second later my plane is rocked by two shells bursting in front of me and two behind me. Boom! Boom! Boom! Boom! The black clouds erupted practically in my face and "Jamie Boy" was rocked and shook like hell. There were German 88 mm flak guns in each corner of the field. I had been fired on many times but that was the first time that I ever heard the flak bursts. The gunners had my range perfect and that was on their first shot. I put "Jamie Boy" into a dive to change my altitude and tried to get the hell out of there. Everyone scattered, but they were tracking me. They fired again and again. My plane was rocked like mad and I could hear that quad "Boom! Boom! Boom! Boom!" of anti-aircraft explosions. They tracked me like that, firing away until I was out of range and I tell you, that was a close one. They were good crews. That time they not only had surprise but they also had my range perfectly and there were four of them. I had no choice, but to get out of there or get shot down.

Another time, when a solitary gun crew opened up on me, I wasn't going to run from them. I just went into a dive aimed right at them with my machineguns blazing; six .50 caliber guns blasting away at this lone gun crew. Since I was firing tracers, I could see where my bullets were going. I was hitting what I was aiming at. That gun crew never bothered another plane ever again.

We still did bomber escort, but because our P-40s weren't as good as the Spitfire, most of our missions were dive-bombing runs. It was not uncommon for us to fly low-level support for British troops as well as for our own forces. It was a combined arms alliance. As a matter of fact, the anti-aircraft crews at our base were British. We even ate British chow and believe me, it was as bad as ours. Mutton and such, Ugh! One of the British guys we met was a relative of Johnny Walker. He sent us a whole case of scotch. It took a while to get to us and arrived months later when we were in Italy.

After our forces took Sicily, they started up the boot of Italy. My squadron was stationed in Sicily for several months. The Germans were in a constant state of retreat and we never let up on them. We hit them all the way through their retreat and it was extremely rare to even see an enemy plane in the Mediterranean theater. We flew missions in the Adriatic, over Greece, and all over Italy. We shot up and bombed everything that moved along their retreating front. My flights never saw a German fighters but one time while on bomber escort I saw an Italian Macchi. I called Davis and asked for permission to break off and attack the enemy fighter. The Macchi was by himself and he was not attacking us so Davis said, "Hold your position." I know we could have gotten him. We were above him and there would have been two of us, me and my wingman. If it had been my command, since there was no other threat, I would have let someone go get him, but Davis was by the book. We were on bomber escort and we would stay with those bombers, come hell or high water. That Macchi knew he was in danger too because he was scooting like hell out of there. The Macchi was the best fighter the Italians had. It was the only enemy fighter that could out-turn our P-40s. Before then I had never seen an Italian fighter. It was a rare incident and I would never see another.

On August 30, I had to pick up a plane in North Africa, a P-40. I was to fly it back to Sicily. Only when I checked it out, the compass was all out of wack and the mechanics told me it would take at least a day to either fix it or replace it. But I didn't want to sit around in North Africa in August. It was damn hot and the flies were unbearable. It was miserable there. I decided, Hell, I don't need a compass, I'll just wing it. How hard could it be? All I needed to do was head east/northeast. I took off from Tunis and headed in the direction I thought Sicily was. I'd been flying for a while when I began to think, I should be there pretty soon. It was a relatively short flight from Tunis to Sicily, but I couldn't see land anywhere. Then I saw clouds to the left and the right and knew they indicated land. Since, I'd been heading toward what I thought was east/northeast, I figured the clouds on the right were over Sicily. I headed for them. Then I realize the island down there was too small to be Sicily, but I could see an airfield below with planes on it. Since I was starting to get low on fuel, I had to go down and land. I hoped it wasn't German. It

97

turned out to be British held Malta. I had accidentally flown to Malta. It was embarrassing! To land on the wrong damn island. We all had our own little screw ups but going to Sicily and landing on Malta? I gassed up and headed north, but I knew I could never let the others know about this one. If I did, I'd never hear the end of it! They'd probably call me the Maltese Falcon for the rest of my life, or worse. Since I was a flight leader, I covered it up by writing in a scheduled trip there. I told the guys in my squadron that I just wanted to check it out. I was the first Tuskegee airman to land on Malta. I turned this fiasco into a kind of honor. There was never any danger of their shooting at me, either, because since Charlie Hall had shot down that German fighter in July we hadn't seen much enemy aircraft in the Southern Mediterranean. We had complete control of the air. All the German fighters were back protecting their homeland trying to stop the daily and nightly strategic bombing of Germany and their military lifeline, the Ploesti oil fields in Romania. They weren't going to protect Italy while American and British bombers leveled Berlin and turned every other German city into rubble.

In September, Colonel Davis was reassigned to the states where he assumed command of the all black 332 Fighter Group. Operations Officer "Spanky" Roberts took command of the 99th. Erwin Lawrence became the new Operations Officer. Unbeknownst to us, Colonel Davis was called to Washington

D.C. to defend our war record. It's a good thing we didn't know about it. After losing men like Sherman White, it would have been very disheartening. The claims cited against the 99th were that we had failed to gain enough aerial victories. There was no mention of our constant assignments for tactical duty as ground support or as use as dive-bombers, or the complete lack of an enemy air presence. Thankfully, the higher-ups were willing to look at the facts and not listen to the men who were trying, falsely, to discredit us. It helped that expert, white pilots like Colonel Cochran, the dive-bomber commander who we flew with upon our arrival in North Africa, praised the 99th as "a collection of born dive-bombers," but it was Davis' testimony and other African Americans who were responsible for revealing the truth to the politicians.

Meanwhile, we continued to fly a lot of low-level support missions. There was almost no danger from enemy fighters because we had control of the skies, but there was always enemy anti-aircraft. It was important to have airfields close by because over Anzio the enemy Ack-Ack was intense. A lot of times allied planes were shot up but were able to limp back to their airfields if they were close enough. There are very few places in the world worse to crash-land than Italy. It is probably the rockiest, most uneven and unforgiving land in Europe! I had to crash-land there twice so I know. Sicily was also bad! Up to then, for me, the war had been very impersonal.

Sherman was MIA. I kept waiting for him to show up at our base. But everything changed when my best friend Sydney Brooks was killed crash-landing in Sicily on September 18. It happened on his take off.

When we took off we usually went in pairs. Then we'd climb and circle until everyone was airborne, then we'd close into formation. I was the flight leader on that mission. I had already taken off was up flying but I could only count seven planes. I glanced around to see who was missing, then I said over the airway, "What happened to Brooks? Where's Brooks?" The guy who had taken off with him said, "He had trouble." Brooks was like my little brother. I left the pattern and flew back over the airfield and there I saw his plane burning like hell. We were going on a long-range escort mission so we had all our long-range fuel tanks on. Those were directly under our planes, attached where we usually held our bombs. Each drum held 75-gallons of high-octane fuel. And there were two of them! You did not want to land with them on.

Apparently, Brooks had taken off, but he'd had immediate engine trouble. He had wanted to make a forced landing but couldn't find anywhere suitable to do it. He'd been unable to get to a safe altitude to bail out but he was able to circle back around and come in for a landing on our airfield, where he was forced to make a wheels-up landing. It was rough country, even in the smooth areas, and when you land like that it is highly probable that you will pitch forward, tip-over, and find yourself trapped underneath your aircraft. God help you if it's on fire. Brooks was forced to land on his belly, which meant he landed on his fuel drums. There was burning gas everywhere!

I was flying overhead when I saw Brooks bail out of his plane and run away from the flames. Thick black smoke was rising up into the sky in a wide swath. The Army service crews were already racing toward the wreckage with medical personnel and firefighting equipment to help. I thought he was going to be fine. At that point there was nothing I could do anyway because I had to lead B flight on its mission. We were supposed to rendezvous with some bombers for an escort mission, but it was a totally wasted trip because the bombers never showed up. I was anxious to get back and check on Brooks.

When we retuned, I went directly to the hospital base to see him. Brooks was fine. I talked to him. He had been burned badly, but the doctors said he'd be okay. I remembered he was worried about his face. "Your face is fine!" I assured him, "Your goggles and oxygen mask protected you. Your facial burns are minor. You'll be fine!" I went back to my quarters for the night, but before my mission the next day, I went back real early to check on him. When I walked in the next morning, the doctor told me Brooks had died in his sleep from shock. I was devastated! I took his death very hard. We were so close. I had always felt very protective of him. He was like my younger brother. I had taken it upon myself to look out for him while we were overseas. His wife Lucille had been one of my best friends since childhood. We knew each other's families so well. I took Brooks' death very hard. I sat down and wrote Lucille a letter but she never got it. Military sensors intercepted it.

Shortly after Brooks's death, I received word from my family by v-mail that my grandfather had passed away. That was another very sad time. I sat reading the v-mail and saw that the funeral was held two days after the letter was written, but because it took so long for letters to get overseas, that had been several months ago already. I knew I could never have made it back for his funeral anyway. The war wasn't going to wait. People learned of their parent's funeral and were unable to go home for it. That fact didn't make it any easier. I loved my grandfather very much.

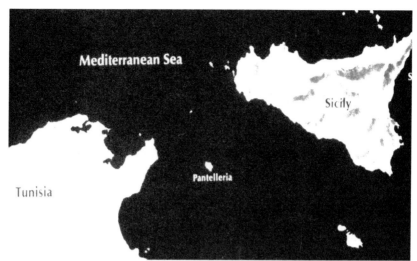

I left Tunis without a compass heading for Sicily in what I thought was an east/northeast direction. Malta is the tiny island just below Sicily, southeast of Pantelleria. Turning my fiasco into an honor, I was the first Tuskegee airman to land on Malta. I just told everybody I wanted to see what it looked like.

ITALY

On the 23rd of September, the 99th Pursuit Squadron left
Sicily for Paestum, Italy. The allies were slowly pushing up the
Italian coast and the 99th was flying low-level support for the
advance as well as occasional bomber escort. On October 17, we
were moved further north to Foggia, Italy, where we remained
for several months.

By mid January of 1944, the 99th was attached to the 79th
Fighter Group. Our primary role was to give air support for the
ground troops fighting in Italy, but soon we would be providing
air cover for a huge allied invasion fleet that would land behind
the German lines. We were moved to Capodichino Air Field
near Naples. Naples was nice, but it was sad. The Germans had
just been there. The people had had it tough and were bent on
just surviving. The women had it the hardest. Most of the men
were away at war; conscripted, imprisoned or killed.

When we Americans came, we were unlike anyone
they'd ever met. We were a big contrast to the German officers.
The Germans had been so arrogant and heavy-handed. I always
tried to conduct myself as an officer and a gentleman and so did
the others in the 99th Pursuit Squadron. As a result, the Italians
welcomed us with open arms. I sometimes felt we were too soft
to be soldiers. The women must have thought the same because

they loved us. They were just fascinated by us - black Americans! Some of our guys picked up the language pretty well, but, like North Africa, because I spoke French, I was always an interpreter since most of the Italians spoke French.

We commandeered a luxurious villa north of the airport and made ourselves quite comfortable. We would get a jeep and run into town at every opportunity. On one of those occasions, my buddy, "Ace" Lawson, introduced me to a very nice family, the DiMaro's. Mrs. DiMaro made the best spaghetti. She refused to let us pay her for it although she would accept some of the things we would "midnight requisition," like spam and sliced bacon. She had four daughters and they were the nicest people. Of the sisters, I remember Carmen DiMaro. She was only sixteen years old but she had studied French and English and was trying to practice her English constantly. Since I was fluent in French, she would talk to me in French all day long. It was fun! They loved to sing to us, too. They all loved to sing and they taught us some of their songs and visa versa. Carmen would sing over and over, "Volare, volare, volare, con li aviator." That translated to, "I like to fly like the aviator." I had done some tinkering on a piano growing up and could play so she would sing it with me playing her piano. We also had a great time teaching them some of the American jazz songs like Nat King Cole's "Straighten up and fly right." It was a great release from the tensions of combat.

One evening, while visiting the DiMaro's, the air raid sirens went off. The younger sister, Annunzio, jumped up with the most frightened look I had ever seen on a child's face. She never said a word; she just dashed for the door, heading for the air raid shelter. Of course, we officers had never been in a city being attacked by German night bombers and just laughed it off. Thankfully, it wasn't much of a raid because we never even heard any bombs. But of the many wartime memories I would retain throughout my life, the vision of Annunzio, and the look of sheer terror on her face, would stay with me for the rest of my life. No child should ever have to feel that kind of fear. All that can be said about war is that it is all bad!

It was always hard to leave the DiMaro's and go back to the war. The girls would beg us to come back and ask us to bring things for them when we returned. We'd appropriate stuff from the mess hall and take big hams and sliced bacon back for them. Every minute we had we tried to get away from the war, get into town. To some of the guys, it was to enjoy wine, women, and song. Some of the guys fell in love with the Italian girls. But for others, like me and Spanky Roberts, being with the Italians was a reminder of family and the things we missed so much back home. The Italians were wonderful people.

On January 22, 1944, Allied Forces landed at Anzio to try to break the stalemate that had developed in the mountains of Italy around Monte Cassino. The invasion had gone well, but instead of exploiting and breaking out in those first early days of the attack, the allied commander ordered his forces to consolidate in the Anzio area. This gave the Germans valuable time to react. They immediately counterattacked and came disastrously close to throwing the allied foothold off Anzio.

On January 25, and 26, I lead flights in the vicinity of Anzio but not over the beachhead. We didn't encounter any enemy aircraft. Then, on January 27, I was leading a flight over the assault beaches when we encountered German fighters. I don't think I would call what happened to me a dogfight, though. I don't know what to call it, but it was fast and furious.

We were flying close air support for allied ground troops over Anzio. We didn't want to fly over the Navy or our Army if we could help it because they fired at anything in the air. The 99th Pursuit squadron was based in Naples, Italy at this time, only ten or fifteen minutes from Anzio. We would patrol in formation, waiting for the radar people to call us up and tell us if they'd picked up anything. With a few exceptions, we hadn't been in much aerial combat for almost six months, not since Charlie Hall had shot down that German fighter last July. And that's simply because there hadn't been any German planes in the air. We knew we didn't have to worry about the Italian Air Force because they were no threat at all. As we are patrolling in formation, my radio crackled, "Red Fox Leader, Red Fox Leader, we have twenty-two bogies closing!" Every one of our guys was listening. We were in a fairly loose formation just kind of tooling around, but once that call came over the radio, Boop! Just like that, we were in one tight formation. I could see all their heads swiveling around in their cockpits, suddenly so alert, looking like crazy for those German Fighters.

I finally saw them and they were real high. I counted 24 of them. We were the low-level support, about 8,000 feet, and the British Spitfires were the high level support, but the British fighters were nowhere to be found. That put the Germans above us, in a much better position. There was no way we could climb to meet them. They weren't interested in us, though. They were already descending from 20,000 feet on their dive-bombing run of our ships and forces on the Anzio beachhead. They were mostly Focke Wolfe 190s with a few Me-109s, all coming from the north. They went into their dive with a turn so that when they finished their run they would be heading back to the north. They passed about 12,000 feet on their way down to the deck and that's when we hit them.

With my flight behind me, I put Jamie Boy into a split S and attacked. If a pilot wants to reverse direction 180 degrees, he does a split S, (half loop) so he is upside down and the turn spits him out in the direction he wants to end up -- in our case, on the tail of the German fighters. It was happening so fast it was unlike anything I had ever seen in all my training. That S turn had spit me out at close to 400 mph. When I came out of my S, however, I couldn't see anything but open sky. No enemy planes, no friendly planes. Nothing. I'm thinking, "Where the hell is everybody?" I was almost on the deck, and then I looked to my side and right there, slightly in front of me was a FW-190. It was almost too good to be true. I only had to maneuver just a little to get in behind him. All this has happened in the span of maybe two seconds, tops. I fired away at him and saw pieces of his plane tear off as I hit him, but he veered and poured on the coals. Their planes were faster than our P-40's so if the German pilot had a cool head, and this flight leader did, he could get away from us. He outdistanced me and they all broke and ran. I got credit for damage, but I didn't see him go down.

Several of our guys were in good positions on the other German fighters because we got six of them on that run before they headed for home. We engaged a greater number of enemy fighters with inferior planes and did it without the loss of even one of our aircraft. Later, back at our airbase in Naples, when I had time to think about the engagement, I thought the German fighters must have been rookies because these pilots we encountered were obviously beginners. One of our guys was relating his kill and he described the action of the German pilot who was obviously panicking. Instead of using his faster plane to just outdistance us, he flew right to left and back until he got blown out of the sky by a slower, inferior aircraft. By this time Germany had lost so many pilots that they were throwing up anyone who could fly. They were really scrapping the bottom of the barrel. The best enemy pilots were defending Germany as we found out later and it's a good thing we got the P-51 Mustang when we did because when our fighters met their best pilots or went up against the Me-262 jet fighter, they needed them.

On a later flight that same day, twelve of our P-40s encountered more enemy fighters. Two more German planes were shot down (one by Erwin Lawrence) and two additional probables were scored. January 27 was our most successful day to date: eight confirmed German fighters destroyed, two probables, and four damaged. It was a great day. But our successes were tempered by the loss of Sam Bruce. He was another MIA who never came back. Like Sherman, we heard rumors, but we never knew what happened to him.

January 28 was another good day. Two flights of our P-40s encountered four Me-109s and three Focke Wulf 190s. Charlie Hall shot down two more enemy planes and two other pilots got one each for a total of four enemy aircraft for the day.

For months we had been criticized for not racking up enemy kills. But how could we? We rarely saw any German fighters and when we did, there were always twenty of us against three or four of them so they never dared to engage us and always ran away. Over Anzio, however, the Germans rushed the Luftwaffe in to try to stop the invasion and we got the chance to prove ourselves. The 99th was flying with the British

Spitfires, the British 75th Squadron, and Colonel Cochran's Red Guerillas (an American P-40 Warhawk Squadron like ourselves) against over one-hundred German fighters. In engagements with the enemy, the tally of shot-down German fighters since the Anzio invasion began was this: The Red Guerillas shot down five German fighters; the British 75th Squadron got one; the British Spitfires got nine; the 99th Pursuit Squadron shot down twelve.

I was never in a high altitude battle with a German fighter. I don't think you could call the engagements I was in classic dogfights. In 67 missions I only encountered German fighters twice. But the two times I encountered them were unlike any other experience I have ever been involved in. They were incredibly fast! I don't know how to explain them other than to say they were hairy. You don't have any room to maneuver when you're at the low altitudes that we flew at so you are dodging in and out of trees, ducking up and down small rises. It's quite a rush at almost 400 mph. One slip up and you crash into a mountain or something.

We flew daily missions around Anzio but it was turning into a mess down there. The allied ground forces were bottled up on the beachhead, fighting, not to breakout anymore, but to simply stay alive. We flew low level air support for the ships and the ground troops. Without us, the ground troops would have been hard pressed.

With all the anti-aircraft fire, from both sides, crash-landing was always a concern. My first crash landing was in Italy and it was due to mechanical difficulties. We were based out of Naples and I had engine trouble at about 1,000 feet. Jamie Boy was blowing thick, black clouds of smoke, but luckily there were no flames. I lost altitude, but wasn't able to bail out as I intended, so I spotted the flattest piece of land below me and just bellied in to a farmers pasture. I walked away without a scratch and we were able to save Jamie Boy. They sent a tank repair vehicle in and towed him out. That first crash landing wasn't nearly bad as my next belly landing. That was when I tangled with four German fighters.

On February 5, I was leading my flight of seven P-40s (one of our planes had engine trouble and had to go back) when we encountered twelve German Me-109s and Fw-190s. The German fighters were flying low, at 1,000 feet, heading for our ships. We were at about 6,500 feet, and right at that moment, I remembered an old ghetto expression, "If you want to kick ass, you got to bring ass." I said, "Let's go," and we dove on them. Both sides moved in for the kill.

An aerial battle is a wild mess. That is why it's called a dogfight! That is exactly what it is- a frenzied, rabid, wild, swirling mess in the sky. Everyone is firing and maneuvering for position. Bullets are everywhere! Tracer's crisscross the sky and any resemblance of a formation disintegrates the moment combat begins. After the first screaming run at each other, usually going head to head, flight leaders try to get into position for the kill while the wingman attempt to stay with them. Things happen so fast. You come out of a run and there's no one in sight but then suddenly you are right behind somebody. Often, you're suddenly flying with someone that isn't your wingman. One of our guys thought he was joining a buddy and found himself behind a Focke Wolf. He quickly realized it and fired but the 190 had noticed it first and got away.

The ground forces, both friend and foe, were blazing at everything in the air and within a few wild seconds planes are spread out all over the sky in mass confusion. On this engagement, with my wingman on my tail, we went head to head with four German fighters. At least, that's what I thought was happening.

Unbeknownst to me, at that exact moment, my wingman, 1ˢᵗ Lieutenant George McCrumby, had been shot down by anti-aircraft fire. I had no idea as I went headlong into four 190s that I was attacking alone! I thought McCrumby was right with me. I opened up with a burst of fire from Jamie Boy on the German flight leader. We both passed going over 350 mph each and then maneuvered for positioning. I got in behind one of the Fw-190s and I saw my tracers tear into him, but then, to my shock, one of my .50's jammed, followed quickly by another and another. I watched in mounting horror as the last of my guns jammed. I was unarmed, fighting against four superior aircraft. I looked frantically for my wingman, but I couldn't see him. I knew I was dead if I didn't get out of there, so I wheeled around to find anyone to help me. We always trained that way and it was just instinctive to look for another P-40, clip onto him, and regroup. Two single planes would pair off, regroup with another guy or guys, and soon the entire flight was together again. At least, that is what is supposed to happen, but that day, all organization in the sky had disintegrated. The other guys were spread out, fighting for their lives, and there was nobody close. There were only six of us now (my wingman had been shot down) fighting against twelve German fighters. But they must have been trying to stay alive too because all I saw were swastikas swarming the air around me. I couldn't see a single friendly plane. Unarmed, I knew it was time to get the hell out of there, or die!

I turned back for Anzio, knowing I would rather risk anti-aircraft fire than these German machineguns, when out of my peripheral vision, I saw the German flight leader come in after me. He was real aggressive and followed me down toward the beachhead. Usually our anti-aircraft was enough to scare anyone away but not this guy. I was desperate, that was the only reason I went there. It was dangerous to fly over Anzio under any flag. Ground fire had already got my wingman and there's no guarantee it was enemy fire either. But this German flight leader wanted my ass bad. He was right behind me, flying a superior, faster plane and firing away. I could see his tracers whipping and knifing past my fuselage and wings. I was flying between mountains, over small rises and hills, and even between trees, doing everything I could to shake him. Everything was happening so fast. I had never been in this bad a situation. His tracers were stabbing by and I knew he was lining me up with that 37mm cannon in the nose of his plane. I said to myself, "Uh-oh, here comes that cannon."

I wheeled about and broke hard and sure enough, he fired just then. I saw the ground explode a couple of hundred yards in front of me where his shell hit a hill. Seconds before his tracers had been flying horizontally past me, now white lines of fire were also rising vertically as we took anti-aircraft fire from the ground. It was hairy! I was worried I was going to burn up my engine trying to get away but I had no choice. I had to do anything I could to get away. With mounting fear I noticed I was losing altitude. I looked back to see where the 190 was but he must not have liked that anti-aircraft fire because he had turned for home. I breathed with relief that he was not behind me but now I had a new problem. I was losing power and altitude. I didn't think he had hit me, but I wasn't sure. I thought I had burned up my engine trying to get away. I realized I was not going to make it back to Naples because I was losing power too fast. I tried to gain altitude to bail out but I couldn't even reach 500 feet so I found the best spot I could, leveled off,

115

kept my flying speed up so I wouldn't stall, and came in for a belly landing out in a pasture. That was the most frightening part of the entire experience.

If you ever want to feel fear, try a belly landing. Even after all that, the time I was most afraid was coming in for that belly landing on that rocky Italian soil. I went from gliding in smooth air, to slamming into planet earth, without the benefit of tires, and I did it at a speed of over 100 mph. It was the adrenaline rush of my life. Rocks and debris flew up my sides; it sounded like a freight train was roaring right by my ear and the noise of screeching metal on rock was deafening. I went several hundred yards, bouncing and grating against rocks, before the nose of the plane dug a trench into the ground and the back shot way up into the air. Jamie Boy decelerated to a complete halt and I was thrown forward against my instrument panel as my canopy slammed shut. The jolt knocked the hell out of me. It took me a second to regain my senses. I was terrified of burning alive and expected Jamie Boy to burst into flames. I was lucky my canopy didn't jam because that was always a pilots fear if his plane is on fire. I got out quickly and luckily Jamie Boy wasn't on fire.

I looked around to assess my situation and had absolutely no idea where I was. I had been over the German lines when the dogfight began so I was a little worried. As I stood in the middle of this field, I saw a farmhouse about 300 yards away. In the opposite direction from the farm house, I could see some soldiers approaching. There were four of them and I recognized them as American. They get up closer and I could see they were rangers, all enlisted men. They saw that I was black and were surprised. I said, "What took you so long?" One of the guys laughed and said, "You see that farmhouse over there. That's a German outpost. We were waiting to see if they were coming to get you. We thought you were German." I was very relieved to see them. The Ranger added, "We've been watching the dog fights."

I had gone down in the middle of no-mans land. Luckily the Germans hadn't come out for me; otherwise I'd be dead or a prisoner of war. The rangers led me back to their lines and I had a memorable evening at their outpost. I was the only officer there. The Rangers asked me where I was from and we had some vino. We sat around talking, but I had just survived a dogfight and a crash-landing so I mostly listened, my thoughts to myself. I stayed at that Ranger outpost for a few hours until a jeep arrived to take me back to Anzio where I stayed the night on the beachhead airstrip. I had to sleep on the ground and we were taking an incredible bombardment of mortar and artillery fire. The ground shook. The explosions were deafening. Looking around, I saw the dark night was lit by an eerie yellow sheen from the multiple, pulsating explosions. It seemed as if the ruined city was on fire. Anzio beachhead was not a good place to be. I suddenly had a new appreciation for ground troops. That was the worst night of my life. I said to myself, "This [infantry] is not for me!"

I flew back to my squadron in Naples the following morning. When I got back, one of the first guys I ran into was my wingman George McCrumby. We both asked, "What happened to you?" He answered first.

"I had a hell of a time," he said, still noticeably fazed. "I thought I was a dead man. Anti-aircraft fire hit me. My plane just flipped. It was a miracle I wasn't killed." As he talked, I noticed his eyes. They were bloodshot from the slip-stream and almost bright red. "I was thrown out of the plane, but my leg was caught in the cockpit. My body was slapped around and slammed against the fuselage. It's amazing I wasn't knocked unconscious. Then the plane flipped again and this time I was thrown clear. Thank God my chute opened."

He was damn lucky he didn't get killed as he descended in his parachute through all the bullets and ground fire. We'd heard the German ground troops shot pilots in parachutes. I don't know if its true, but we'd even been told that German pilots shot at parachutes, too. I couldn't even imagine one of our pilots doing that. From what we witnessed on the ground, though, when we moved into areas where the Germans had just pulled back, I wouldn't be surprised by anything they did. The Germans were just ruthless.

I told my wingman what happened to me and some of the other guys came around to listen. All my buddies were glad to see me but they were also disappointed to have to give all my stuff back. When I hadn't returned, they thought I was dead. They had already wrote me up as a KIA and divided up my stuff. Davis was getting ready to write my wife. When I walked into my billet, everything was gone. I said, "Where is my cot? Where is all my stuff?" I had to scrounge everything back. I was irritated. I couldn't blame the guys, though, that was the way things were done in wartime. When Brooks died, his wife Lucille was the best cook and she frequently sent him cookies and brownies. Brooks still received packages for weeks until his wife was notified. [viii] The packages of goodies kept arriving for Brooks. We thought, "He'd want us to have them." We weren't going to just throw them away or let them go to waste. So we all shared his stuff. Life always goes on.

The battle for Italy continued. I received a new plane. There would be no recovering Jamie Boy. He was now beyond the front line and his fuselage was literally ripped to shreds. It was tough losing Jamie Boy. He'd been my plane all across North Africa, Sicily and through all my Italian missions.

The day I crash landed, Elwood Driver, one of the guys in my flight, shot down a German Fw-190, raising our total of enemy kills, since Anzio began, to thirteen. Then on February 7 we got three when Wilson Eagleson, Leonard Jackson and Clinton Mills each got one, raising the tally to sixteen. We would probably have been even more successful during those first few weeks of February had the German fighters come to fight. They almost always broke and ran at the first sign of allied fighters.

Our successes were getting noticed. General Henry "Hap" Arnold, the commander of the Army Air Forces, wrote of us, "The results of the 99th Fighter Squadron during the past two weeks, particularly since the Nettuno landing, are very commendable."

I read in the Stars and Stripes that a black infantry outfit was fighting in Italy. It was my brother Thurston's unit. I found out later, after the war, that my brother knew where I was because of all the publicity we were getting, but I had no idea where he was, other than we were in the same country.

After I completed my 65th mission, I qualified to return home. I was anxious to get home because my daughter Michal was going to be a year old and I'd never seen her. Dryden saw my daughter before I did. He went home in September, the day after Brooks died. Dryden didn't rotate home; instead went back to train the 332nd. When they were ready he'd come back over. Dryden sent me a picture of his wife "Pete" holding my daughter Michal, who I'd still never seen.

I was anxious to go home but once I got that 65th mission, I couldn't just pack my belongings and fly home. I had to keep flying missions until they were able to rotate me back, filling my spot with a replacement. Fortunately, Colonel Davis was back in command, having returned with the vanguard of the 332 that were newly arrived in Italy flying the dreaded P-39 aerocobras, and he knew I hadn't seen my little girl. Colonel Davis gave me a break and let me rotate back home after serving only two additional missions.

Some guys stayed on and volunteered for extra missions. Usually that was for a promotion. My friend Erwin Lawrence stayed and was promoted to major and then again to squadron commander. He flew over 100 combat missions. He was killed flying a P-51 Mustang over Greece. His plane was hit by anti-aircraft and went into the ground at over 400 mph.

BACK TO THE STATES, March 1944

When I received word that I was going home, I was so excited that I would finally get to see my wife and daughter. I wanted to leave immediately. The quickest way to get home was for me to fly myself, but there were so many veterans rotating home that they put us on a troop ship. It was a brand new ship on its maiden voyage and it was full of combat veteran pilots, bombardiers, tail gunners and navigators.

The average American probably doesn't understand why the Army Air Corps combat veterans got to rotate home while the Navy and Army infantry and tank crews had to stay on for the duration. One reason was because of mortality rate. They needed to give the men flying these dangerous missions a reason to go on. If they had a goal to reach -- a number of missions that could send them back home -- it would keep morale up. Most American's don't know that the Strategic Bombing Campaigns of the Second World War suffered higher casualties than any other service, including infantry, put together. More men were killed in the air than on the ground and at sea and that includes North Africa, Sicily, Italy, France, Germany and the countless islands in the Pacific. That seems hard to believe but there were daily bombing missions in all theaters of war. Hundreds of planes would take off daily full of crewmen. Some of those missions over Germany were thousand plane raids. Each bomber had a crew of two pilots, a navigator, a bombardier, a radioman and several gunners. That was a lot of men. A B-25 medium bomber had a twelve man crew. Add the long range escort fighter pilots on those missions and you have thousands of men in aerial combat every day. Sometimes a third of the bombers would not return. The casualties were horrendous. There were rarely survivors in a plane crashes.

To give an example, our unit was relegated to missions in an area with an almost non-existent German air presence. Of the 99th's twenty-four plane squadron, we lost Sherman White, James McCullum, Paul Mitchell, Sidney Brooks, Sam Bruce, Alwayne Dunlap, Erwin Lawrence and several others. That is more than twenty-five percent casualties. Not one of those men was killed by enemy aircraft. Engine malfunctions, mid air collisions and enemy anti-aircraft were the killers. Flying is inherently dangerous.

It was the survivors of these dangerous missions who were on board this new ship, headed for home. Because of the danger of German U-Boats, everyone was immediately assigned a responsibility during "battle-stations" in case of emergency. As an officer, I had the assignment of cutting the ropes at the raft stations and throwing the rafts overboard.

As we were cruising out into the Atlantic where the U-Boats were still raising hell, we wondered where our escort was.

123

We had no aircraft, no destroyers, nothing. We voiced our concern but they told us not to worry because supposedly this new ship was so fast it could outrun any U-Boat. We weren't very reassured but what could we do about it. And besides, there was probably not a man aboard ship that would have stayed in Italy when presented with the chance to get home.

We left Naples, and were not more than a day out of Italy when we got word that a German submarine was shadowing us. The ship full of combat vets, all rotating home after completing months of dangerous missions, are none to happy about this news. But the crew kept reassuring us that the ships speed would protect us. Then, two days out, alone in the middle of the Atlantic Ocean, at night, tailed by a German sub -- and the ship came to a dead halt. The engines on that brand new ship broke down. It was panic time!

All hell broke loose on that ship. It was the middle of the night so absolute black-out was ordered. There were no lights, not even a lit cigarette, unless you want to get torpedoed. That was scary because the first thing a nervous smoker wanted to do was light up to steady his nerves. In 1943, seemingly everybody smoked and we were all scared as hell. Everyone was running around on the deck of that ship, trying to do their job or get to their battle station, but they were bumping into one another, getting lost in the dark and making way too much noise. Even the crew was unfamiliar with the ship because it was its maiden voyage. The captain was apoplectic as the crew scrambled to try to restart the engine. As I waited at my battle station for the order to start cutting the ropes and throw the life rafts over, all I could think about was that I had survived 67 combat missions, only to die on a transport bound for home. I'm sure there wasn't a combat veteran on that boat who didn't share those thoughts. That was one of the longest nights of my life, second only to the night I spent at Anzio. In the morning they were able to restart the engines and we continued on our way toward New York. We found out later that someone had accidentally put ocean water into the oil -- a typical snafu.

When we arrived in New York, I was immediately shipped to a redistribution center in Atlantic City, New Jersey. The pilots went there. All their families were waiting and there was a lot of excitement and happiness. My wife had taken the train from Ohio and she was waiting for me. I was a captain then and word had spread around that a black fighter pilot from the 99th was returning home from the war and that his wife was meeting him. I was the only black officer to rotate home at that time. With the other returning veterans, I had orders to stay at a military hotel. As my wife and I walked out of the distribution center, I was carrying all our bags-- two large suitcases and two smaller bags. We were staying at a real plush hotel in Atlantic City where all the combat vets stayed upon their return home. It was a sort of military hotel for the time being. The commander in charge of the hotel, a full bird colonel, came rushing over to me and grabs our bags. I'm just a little captain, and a full bird colonel was carrying my bags. I said, "That's okay, Colonel. Thank you, I can get them." He refused and insisted on carrying our bags in and he was so gracious. He bent over backwards to make my wife and I feel welcome. We were the only black couple in the hotel. He was such a gentleman. It was embarrassing he was so nice. We really appreciated it because we had our share of horror stories, suffered simply because of our skin color.

After that brief time in Atlantic City, Phyllis and I returned to Cincinnati, Ohio where I saw my daughter for the first time. Michal was two and she was beautiful. I had two enjoyable weeks at home before my orders came. I was to return to Tuskegee and become a fighter instructor. I went back to Alabama and found life stateside wasn't too much different than it had been overseas. I was still flying for the Army Air Corps, only now instead of flying combat missions over Europe, I was a fighter instructor at Tuskegee.

It was neat to be back in Tuskegee and see the many classes passing through. Dryden and I were all that was left from class 42-D, the second class. I ran into Dryden's wife "Pete" who was a nurse at the Tuskegee Military hospital. She told me that Dryden was assigned to a base in South Carolina, getting ready to return to Europe with the 332nd. Pete said she tried to drive down to see him as much as she could, and Dryden tried to fly up to Tuskegee every chance he got. Since I had the weekends off, the very next Friday I decided I'd save Pete the drive and fly her to South Carolina to surprise Dryden.

Pete and I took off in a trainer that I signed for and as we got close to South Carolina, I noticed the gas gauge wasn't working right. I decided that when I landed, I'd have a mechanic look at it. We landed but before I could even taxi in, I ran out of gas on the runway. "Oh my god!" The fuel indicator still read half full, but it was completely empty. Pete was a little surprised, too. I was so thankful I hadn't run out of gas in the air. It was embarrassing to run out of gas on the runway but I was just happy that Pete and I were alive. Dryden never let me hear the end of that.

At Tuskegee, I was a fighter instructor for just a few months until I was reassigned to bomber training. Just like the 99th had been the first African American fighter pilots, I was to join the fledgling 477th Bomber Group which was being organized because of political pressure.

Again, this is how stupid segregation is. It costs millions of dollars to open up a base, to construct the buildings and hangers to house the men and aircraft, get instructors and to do everything else it takes to start a bomber group from scratch. There were already dozens of airfields across the country with the capability and capacity to take these black airmen and turn them into pilots, but none did because of segregation. It was just stupid.

From Tuskegee I went to Douglas Army Airfield in Douglas, Arizona, where I began training in B-25 medium bombers. I didn't particularly like flying a bomber. It was like driving a semi-truck after driving a sports car. It was a large, slow, lumbering, target in the sky. It wasn't entirely without excitement, though. We practiced our bombing runs and it was challenging to hit our targets dead on. We also practiced flying low level ground support, flying B-25s armed with a 75mm nose cannon. The plane rocked from the recoil of the cannon firing. To fire a cannon from the nose of a bomber, and hit what you're aiming at, you have to be at a pretty low altitude. For such a slow aircraft, that is a dangerous mission.

After Douglas, Arizona, we were transferred to Lockbourne Airfield in Columbus, Ohio, where we continued bomber training. From Lockbourne, we were transferred to Godman Field near Fort Knox, Kentucky. To me that was great news because when I had left for North Africa over a year before, my wife had moved back to Cincinnati, Ohio. There was no reason for her to stay in Tuskegee without me. I was from Cleveland, but she was from Cincinnati. With Cincinnati being right on the Kentucky boarder, I was able to go home once a week. The drive, though, was murder, so each weekend I'd requisition a fighter and fly home. I'd land at Lunken Field, the municipal airport, and park my P-40 for the weekend. Then my wife or someone else would come pick me up. Now, to let them know that I was in range and someone should head to the airport, I'd buzz the house. Even back in the forties, there were ceilings when flying over a city, but I'd come down anyway, breaking all the rules. I'd come screaming in waving my wings to let my wife know to send someone to pick me up. [ix] All the neighbors thought it was really something to see a fighter plane come screaming in like that. Apparently, it shook the hell out of the houses. One time my wife was laughing when she picked me up. She told me what had just happened when I buzzed the house. My daughter Michal was playing jacks on the back porch with a little boy when I came over. The little boy was all excited to see a P-40 come screaming down. He was pointing and shouting, "A fighter plane! A fighter plane!" My daughter doesn't even look up. She just says, "Nah, that's just my dad!"

A couple of times I made it back to Cleveland to see my mom and dad. The only thing bad about going home to Cleveland was that I had to see the families of my friends who were killed in action. Both Brooks and Erwin Lawrence were from Cleveland. There families were desperate for information and wanted to know what had happened. I feared the meeting. They asked me to confirm the rumors they had heard. Brooks' family had been told that after bailing out of his plane over the Mediterranean Sea, that Brooks had been killed and eaten by sharks. I couldn't believe it. Who could come up with something so terrible and tell it to a man's family. The censorship of all military information was just so screwed up. I told Lucille exactly what happened, that Sidney had died after a freak accident belly-landing and that he had died of shock in his sleep, painlessly.

The worst was when I went to see Erwin Lawrence's mother. I didn't even want to go see her, but I'd been told that she really wanted to see me. I owed it to Erwin, but I knew it would be horrible. Mrs. Lawrence completely broke down, sobbing and sobbing. It was a bad moment for me. I felt so bad for this poor woman, partly because I had a child. Erwin was Mrs. Lawrence's only son. She only had one other daughter. Erwin was such a great guy too, the nicest guy. He was a handsome, dashing guy. Mrs. Lawrence was so proud of her squadron commander, fighter-pilot son. It was terrible. Erwin's grave was in some farmer's field in Greece until the Army moved him to a military cemetery, on Greece. Mrs. Lawrence tried to have Irwin's body returned home for burial, but the Pentagon refused to ship him home. She would have needed enormous political pressure to do that because so many American families wanted the bodies of their sons brought home. If the government did it for one, they'd have to do it for everyone.

I returned to Fort Knox and continued bomber training. By that time I'd made captain and was one of the senior black officers. James Wiley and a few other guys had also rotated back, but of the bomber pilots, since I had been in the second class at Tuskegee, I was the most senior. Even though we were still segregated, we were training at Fort Knox so we were among white soldiers and airmen. The only time in my entire military service when I was treated without the respect due my rank, was at Fort Knox.

I was walking across the parade ground, heading for the PX, and a private was going the other way. There was nobody else around and it seemed we were the only two on the whole base. Our paths took us right past each other. This young private, a white kid, walked by me without saluting. He saw me, no doubt about it. He couldn't have missed me. I was a captain and a veteran, back from the war with combat ribbons on my chest and this young punk wouldn't salute me. He got maybe one step past me before I lost it.

"SOLDIER!" I roared, whirling around, "Don't you recognize an officer when you see one!" He immediately turned and snapped to attention. I could see by the fear on his face that he knew he'd made a very big mistake. I was so mad I could barely control myself. I'd never been so angry. I balled my fist and put it up right in front of his mouth. "There's no one here but you and me," I snarled, "I'll break your goddamn face." His

131

eyes were wide in fear and his pale cheeks turned beat red. He immediately saluted. I saluted back and said, "Dismissed." He put his tail between his legs and moved quickly away, but as I thought about it, I was afraid of what I might have done. All the years of suppression might have exploded into one savage beating. I was very glad that didn't happen.

We continued our very rigorous training at Fort Knox. I had one very close call flying B-25's at Godman Field. I lost an engine just after takeoff. I had a full crew and a full load of fuel. I had to quickly close down the bad engine and feather the prop to reduce the drag on that side. I managed to climb a few hundred feet and circled to come back in for a landing. It was close. I never once reached 500 feet. My crew was sweating bullets, but we came in just fine and landed smooth.

As our training continued, we grew, and it became obvious we needed a bigger airfield and more billets. To accommodate our swelling numbers, we were ordered to Freeman Field in Seymour, Indiana.

FREEMAN FIELD, 1945

The 477th Bomber Group reported to our new airbase at
Freeman Training Field, in Seymour, Indiana. All that can be said
about Seymour was that it had nice long runways. Other than that
it was like being stranded on an island. It was isolated and there
was nothing to do. We settled into life at Seymour, met our
instructors, and began training. It just so happened I was the senior
black officer. There were only five pilots that could have been
senior to me anyway, and none of them were at Freeman Field.
There were several other combat veterans, eight or ten from the
99th Pursuit squadron that followed after me, and were put into B-
25 training along with me, to form the combat nucleus for the
group. They wanted veteran leadership because the 477th Bomber
Group was to be sent to Japan as part of the strategic bombing
campaign. Until that time, there hadn't been enough black pilots
to form a bomber squadron. But with more black pilots coming
through Tuskegee, we soon had enough to fill the three squadrons
necessary to compromise a group.

As the senior officer, I was caught right in the middle of an
event that could have ruined my career. I never would have
believed that after all my combat duty, I'd have to go through
something like this back home. The white papers called it "The
Freeman Mutiny." I don't believe that application was accurate at
all. What happened was this: There were two sets of officers

clubs, one for the white instructors and one for the black trainees. The black trainees were not allowed in the white officers club. There were eight of us who were combat veterans, and some of us had been fighter instructors before we were sent to be the combat nucleus of the 477th Bomber Group, yet they lumped us in with all the trainees fresh out of Tuskegee. None of the instructors were combat vets. I was a captain at the time. I'd flown sixty-seven combat missions in Europe. I'd also been a fighter instructor and then a bomber pilot since I got back from Europe. I was nobody's trainee. Who were they to lump me in with the trainees? But they did.

The trouble began when some of the black officers went over to the white officers club for drinks. They thought it was unjust to prohibit an officer of the United States Army Air Corps from entering an officers club. They were right, of course, but not long after that, a memo came out, a special order signed by the colonel, ordering us not to use the officers building. The language was quiet clear.

Truth to tell, I didn't give a damn. My wife was in Ohio and I'd drive over on the weekends to see her. I had a little three-year old daughter I hadn't seen for two years. The last thing in the world I wanted to do was shoot the breeze and drink beer with a bunch of rear-echelon instructors who had never seen combat. Furthermore, the officers building and the trainee officers building were both dives, equally as bad. However, the fact that one was for white officers and the other for black officers was upsetting. It was the principle of the thing. As an officer of the United States Army Air Corps, who'd put his life on the line for his country, why couldn't I use a United States Army Officers club? It was a slap in the face. No, it was worse. It defiled the graves of American men like Irwin Lawrence, Sidney Brooks, and Sherman White, men who'd made the ultimate sacrifice for their country but couldn't get into a dive club because of their skin color.

I wasn't even interested in going to the damn place. But the young guys, stuck over the weekend in little Seymour, Indiana, in a restricted place, were bored to death. There were over one-hundred officers. Young men full of energy and -- in the face of injustice -- absolutely itching for a fight. You couldn't help but hear the murmurings. Since I was the ranking officer, they asked me "Jamison, what are you going to do?" I said, "Where is it?" meaning the club, and they showed me. I went over, entered, looked around, and left. Nothing happened. Nobody questioned me. Then other officers did the same. Some went in small groups and sat for a while. Still nothing happened. It was an episode that developed over a few weeks time and since all the black trainees became aware of it and felt we were being discriminated against, they went more frequently.

The white commander, Colonel Robert Selway, was trying to decide what to do and after more and more guys started going in, Selway simply closed the club down. We weren't causing trouble; the guys just went in for a beer. They closed it, though, until they could come up with a solution. Once in a while, in the evenings, they'd try to open it, but we'd come over. We wanted Selway to back down because we knew what he was doing was illegal. We had a few officers who had gone to law School. We were still in the atmosphere of segregation, but there was an Army War Department regulation that held an anti-discrimination clause so we felt we had the right as officers not to be discriminated against. I'm sure the white commander thought our conduct was unbecoming of an officer, though, because the army still had a segregation policy.

When the commander saw this situation was not going to go away, he put out a new order. As a result, I almost got put under arrest, which could have ruined my career. I wasn't worried about it, though. It was easy to stand up to something like this. The whole idea was intolerable. We were all U.S. officers but it also galled me that these white officers weren't combat veterans. But as I said before, there was no color in combat. If these men had been veterans, or if Selway had been a combat veteran himself, I doubt there ever would've been a problem.

Selway's order named the buildings that were instructor officer buildings and which were trainee officer buildings. By doing so, Selway appropriated new quarters so the black trainee officers would have their own building. The result was that the NCOs base-wide lost their club and had nowhere to go. My squadron commander was a captain, an Italian guy, and he and I were friends. He knew I was a combat vet. I could see the embarrassment on his face. He said, "Captain Jamison, I have a letter from the base commander. We want every officer to read the letter and sign it." I read it over quickly and saw it was going to mean trouble, but I noticed at the end of the letter it read, "I certify that I have read and understand this order." I saw immediately the order was setting us up for a court-martial because we felt obliged to disobey the order. I read it and said, "I'm sorry, captain. I can't sign that. It reads, 'I read and understand,' but I don't understand it." He didn't know what to do. His orders were to have us all sign the paper. "Well, I'll correct this," I told him. I simply lined through "understand," and signed the paper. It read, "I certify that I have read ...the letter." My buddy Jack Rodgers did the same thing -- he ended up becoming a lawyer and a judge. Our entire group signed the paper that way. Usually we talked about what was happening and had time to plan our countermoves, but this time we all just did it. Even still, we were worried. This was during time of war and I didn't want to get in trouble -- it would have been big trouble. The base commander was a full bird colonel, one step from a general. Some of the others signed like me, but a lot of guys wouldn't sign anything at all. The colonel ordered them to sign the next day and it came down to the point that If they didn't sign it, they'd be under arrest. It became a showdown.

After Selway issued these orders, the white officers club opened. The eight of us who had been in combat hoped there would be some bad PR when the public found out that combat vets couldn't use certain facilities just because they were black. We hoped that would be enough to make the colonel back down. It wasn't! Selway barred all newspaper reporters from the base. He then had all firearms removed from the African American MPs, but not the white MPs.

Selway and the others tried to argue that color had no basis in the argument. They tried to mask it, saying it was an issue of instructor vs. trainee. Selway also had the backing of General Frank Hunter, the commander of the 1st Air Force. With his approval, and behind that argument, they began arresting the offending black officers. Not everyone was arrested the same day.

As the senior black officer, I promptly went into the club. One of our black lieutenants, Bill Terry, also went into the white club, but the OD (officer of the day) motioned for him to stop at the door. He said, "You can't come in!" The lieutenant slipped past him and the OD claimed Terry had "bumped" into him. Lieutenant Terry was placed under arrest. The white newspapers said his crime was that he had disobeyed a direct order and jostled a superior officer. A black newspaper reported that, "One hundred and three black officers were placed under arrest for refusing to comply with segregation order and using white officers club." Regardless of the paper you read, Bill Terry was fined $150 dollars, court-martialed, and forced to live as a convicted felon for the next fifty years of his life.

I was never arrested, but the guys who didn't sign that order were arrested the moment they walked in the club. It turned into a huge mess. All flying and training for the 477th Bomber Group came to a complete halt on April 12, 1945. There was a military investigation and Congressmen were involved. All the while the war was raging as we sat around playing cards. There was so much disruption that the entire outfit was flown back to Fort Knox, a field too small for our bomber group to successfully train on. The situation deteriorated so badly that Colonel Davis was called back from the war to take command of the outfit.

I believe this injustice was instrumental in the future desegregation of our armed forces by Truman in 1948. Meanwhile, as we sat idle, Germany surrendered on May 5, 1945 and then Japan surrendered almost four months later, after atomic bombs were dropped on Hiroshima and Nagasaki. The 477th Bomber Group never saw action. It was mired in bigotry back in the United States and prevented from doing its part.

Black Ex-Bomber Pilot's 1945 Conviction Reversed

Associated Press

Los Angeles

Fifty years after he and 61 other black officers marched into a whites-only officers club, Bill Terry's conviction for "jostling" a superior has been reversed.

The 1945 incident helped hasten the desegregation of the military, and became a rallying point in the early civil rights movement.

But Terry, 74, has paid a heavy price. On every loan application, every job application, he has had to acknowledge that he is a convicted felon.

Mysteriously, he failed the state bar exam as many as 10 times after answering that yes, he was a felon — a question the State Bar considers carefully in admissions.

"The crux of it was I was a felon," Terry said. "It didn't matter at first – they didn't shoot me or anything. But when you went to get a job, they'd ask. Year after year, it really did cost."

Terry, then an Army lieutenant and bomber pilot, along with the other members of the 477th Bomber Group — the first black bomber unit — were transferred from Godman Field, Ky., to Freeman Field, Ind. to prepare for possible deployment to the war in the Pacific. It was March, 1945.

Two years earlier, the War Department had directed all military recreation facilities be desegregated.

But Terry's commander at Freeman, General Frank O'Donnell Hunter, had found a loophole, military historians say.

At the ironically named Freeman, one of the officers' clubs was to be used only by "supervisors." Hunter ordered. The other was for "trainees."

All supervisors happened to be white; all trainees black.

"Pilots with 100 missions were trainees," Terry recalled in an interview with the Los Angeles Times. "Our doctors were trainees. Our dentists were trainees."

The black officers met in secret and decided to simply walk into the club. "I couldn't do anything else," he said. "We were young and we were right."

"The guard just said, 'We don't let niggers in,'" Terry said. So I just went . . . around him."

Three of the 61 involved were court-martialed; a total of 101 were reprimanded. Terry spent the next 87 days in solitary confinement.

Terry, charged with mutiny, treason, disobeying a direct order and conspiracy, was the only one convicted. His crime: "jostling," brushing a superior as he went through the door. He was fined $150 and released.

For the next 50 years, Terry lived his life as a convicted felon, until the Air Force set aside his conviction two months ago.

Seventy four year old Bill Terry was exonerated but sadly after almost fifty years. For fifty years, every time he applied for a job it came up that he was a felon who had been court-martialed and dishonorably discharged from the US Army.

DESEGREGATION

After the war I was transferred to several different posts. Since the war was over, all flight officers had to learn another skill. We still had to keep our status as a flyer but we were required to become skilled at a new job. I chose to go to the Army Finance School in St. Louis Missouri to become an accounting and finance officer. I had a choice between the finance school in Saint Louis, Missouri, and the electronics school at Kessler Field in Biloxi, Mississippi. I had wanted to go to electronics school, but I'd never volunteer to go to Mississippi – the south - when I could go elsewhere. They were lynching blacks in Mississippi. I felt, if you wanted to punish a black person, send them to Mississippi. I probably would have been a good electronics officer, but fate kept me from a totally different career. After finance school in St. Louis, I was transferred to Lockbourne Air Force Base in California.

In July of 1947 my son Clarence Clifford Jamison, Jr., was born. By now Michal was five and Phyllis was adapting well as a military wife, moving from base to base with me.

I was still at Lockbourne when President Truman signed Executive Order 9981 on September 2, which officially desegregated the US Armed Services. At Lockbourne we called it "Operation Polka Dot" because it meant we were to be disbanded and shipped to the various bases across the country. I was

141

transferred first to Castle AFB (Air Force Base) in Merced, California to be the base finance officer. Castle AFB was part of SAC (Strategic Air Command.) I was the first black "flying" officer to be assigned there, although two black administrating officers were already there. My wife was the first black officer's wife on the base. My kids were the first black children.

The other officers and enlisted men always treated me with the respect due my rank. There were thirty or forty people under me, almost all white. We were a cohesive unit. I had a few master sergeants under me who were much more experienced than I was. My 1st Sergeant was Bob Holman, who ran the office. He was older than me and knew everything, but I was the one in charge and my authority was never challenged. At first it was awkward in so much as no one knew what I was like. But then we had our first party. 1st Sergeant Holman's wife, Jen, was as nice as he was. She asked me to dance to break the ice. She was a nice woman and I appreciated the way she treated me. After that everyone relaxed. They liked that I was a quiet, laid back guy. They knew they could have gotten some uptight white officer who could have made their lives miserable. Some of them wrote me cards years after I left. That was over fifty years ago and 1st Sergeant Holman still keeps in touch.

At this party, the kids would dance. I had to laugh. At our black bases, before desegregation, our parties were alive with jitterbugging. This party was so funny because most of these white kids didn't have any rhythm.

It was a good post. My wife Phyllis joined the Officer's Wives Club. Some of the women were very nice but others were upset. Some of them completely ignored my wife. That didn't bother Phyllis. She wasn't going to take anything from anyone. After we had made friends with a few of the couples, we found out later about the consternation caused by Phyllis joining. Our friends told us that the wife of the senior white officer had been approached by several of the junior officer's wives. "What should we do about this black officer's wife trying to join the officer's wives club?" The wife of the senior officer had said to these ladies, "That black officer and his wife have more education and more money than you do. Who are you to say anything?" Apparently that had shut them up. They were a rare few. Most of the white officer's wives were very nice to Phyllis and she always made friends easily.

My family enjoyed California. My mother came to visit us and stayed at our quarters on the base. We were again the only black family in the compound. My mother saw my young son playing with the little white boys and exclaimed "That little bur-head don't even know he's colored."

I moved around a lot after the war. From Castle in August of 1949, I was sent to Korea in May of 1951. My unit was stationed near Seoul but also had a contingent at a base in Japan.

They were the same unit, just split between two bases in two separate countries. We stopped at the base in Japan first. Although I was the base finance officer, I needed flying time so I asked for a flight. Pilots have to fly a certain number of hours within a three month period or their flight status was revoked. I flew a C-47 cargo plane to Korea to pick up the casket of an F-80 pilot who was killed in action making a strafing run. That was my first flight of the Korean War; a round trip to Seoul from Japan. Of all the flying I did, that was the only time I ever carried a casket.

After that flight, I flew in-country and settled in at our base in Korea. My job in Korea was putting payroll information down and computing it. Korea needed finance officers badly. Our base was comprised of tents with no running water, much as our base in North Africa had been. We had to use our helmets to shave in. It was miserably cold in the winter. The good thing about being a pilot, though, was that I had to keep up my flying hours, which meant I could go to Japan. I'd sign for a plane and head off to Japan to get a shower whenever I could and at the same time log some hours flying. There was always someone wanting to go back. I'd give them a ride.

In Korea, in 1952, I was still a captain. I'd been a Captain since 1944. I had been a captain longer than any other Army Air Corps captain in Korea. We were at war with hundreds of captains in-country, maybe even a thousand, and I had been one the longest-- for eight years. I can't say it had anything to do with race, but it was an egregious coincidence. In actuality it was probably because I was a finance officer. Finance officers didn't get promoted. It's not a career with upward mobility like a fighter pilot's. My boss in Korea was a comptroller, a lieutenant colonel. The finance officer is under the comptroller. The comptroller had a fiscal officer, a finance officer, budget officer, and so on. Now, my boss, the comptroller, told Colonel Gabreski, "Sir, Jamison has been a captain longer than any captain in Korea." When the colonel heard that, he was disgusted. He may not have even known about my combat record, though he probably did, but he knew I was a good officer and good at my job. The next week I was a major.

I didn't return to Castle AFB until June of '52. That was a short deployment because I left Castle for Forbes AFB in Topeka, Kansas in August of 1952. I was assigned as an accounting & Finance officer. My family and I lived in housing outside the base and my two children went to a nearby elementary school.

In 1954, the country was going through "Brown vs. Board of Education" in Topeka. The situation was inspired by a young black girl having to walk past an all white school to get to her school. She wasn't allowed to go to the school closer to her home because she was black.

In contrast, my family lived in a suburb and the kids went to the regular school. They were the only black students at the school but there was no problem. The principal of the school, Avondale Elementary, was Merrill Ross and he was one of my best friends. It was interesting because it was a school with a black Principal and only two black children enrolled in the entire school -- my children.

Meanwhile, "Brown vs. Board of Education" was happening just a few miles away, in Topeka. We didn't get directly involved but we couldn't help but hear about it. The whole country heard about it. My wife was in a black sorority so she knew what was going on and a lot of our social life was in Topeka. Our friends who were teachers told us all about it. It was another unfortunate, stupid situation caused by prejudice. To me, Topeka was a strange place, almost like the South, with its segregation.

One of my buddies at Forbes AFB was Major Ed Zeidler, a white officer. He was a big stocky guy, a linebacker type, from Minnesota. We were living outside Topeka at the military officers complex. Phyllis and I went to the officers club dances with Ed and his wife and we did a lot with the Zeidlers. They were neat people. Their son was close in age to my son, who, at the time was almost 6 years old. One day Ed offered to take the kids into Topeka to see a movie. I told him, "You can't take Clifford to Topeka. It's segregated." I wasn't saying, "No", I was just speaking a fact aloud as a reminder to him. Anyway, he didn't think it would be a problem and I didn't really either, and Clifford wanted to go, so I said okay. They didn't have any trouble. It just goes to show how ridiculous it was.

We had a very enjoyable three years in Topeka. I was godfather to the Ross' first child, Karen. My wife went to Washburn University in Topeka and received a BS in education. I attended night school and took more accounting and business courses.

As the finance officer, I saw highly classified, top secret stuff. This was during the Cold War and I was part of Strategic Air Command. I had to sign checks for top secret orders and things I cannot talk about; things that would raise eyebrows; things that were never publicized. Also, since I had to pay men on missions, I had to see the orders justifying the mission. It would scare you. It would scare any thinking, moral person.

I stayed in Kansas for four years before deploying overseas for Wheelus AFB in Tripoli, Libya in November of 1956. In 1958 my flying was confined mostly to administrative flying, personnel, and cargo. Desegregation had been over for ten years by now. Once I was flying a plane load of passengers from Tripoli to Rome. My passengers consisted of military families headed for Europe on vacation. There were quite a few young children among them so I wanted the flight to be an especially good one. The kids were very excited because flying was very new. In the 1950's, most people didn't fly, and those that did rarely flew internationally. You didn't just get in a plane and go places back then. They went by ship in those days.

I took off and the flight went well until I encountered bad weather around Naples. I tried to go around it, but suddenly I heard a loud crash, saw a bright flash, and felt the plane jolt. We had been hit by lightning and I could smell something was wrong. The interior of the plane quickly filled with the acrid odor of fumes. It was obvious we had an electrical fire but just how bad it was I didn't know. Everyone behind me in the plane seemed to go into panic mode, but the engine was fine and the radio continued to function alright. I tried not to show the slightest concern when I announced to the passengers that we were diverting to Naples. I had quite a bit of flying time in bad weather, but that was the only time I'd ever been struck by lighting. We made it down with no further incidents. Mechanics fixed our plane and the next day we continued up to Rome.

On another flight I had to pick up a communications cable. It was a big heavy reel. I worried about its weight. I knew it was also something that couldn't be jettisoned in case we had an emergency. It was too heavy. If it slid to the back of the plane, we'd have real problems. We were all concerned. We picked it up in Casablanca and flew it to Tripoli. It was the same route I had flown almost 16 years earlier and it brought back some powerful memories. About an hour or two out I lost an engine. It was night and I had to feather it in. I called Wheelus AFB and alerted them that we had a problem. They scrambled a couple of jets to escort us back in case we had to crash land. This way, if we had engine trouble, they'd know where we went down. We made it back just fine. That was the danger of flying. All through my career as a safety officer I saw it. Fly a plane long enough and you will see mechanical problems.

While stationed in Tripoli, I heard and read about a young rebel named Mohamar Quadafi. Years later I was surprised when that young man would become the dictator of Libya.

I left Tripoli in April of 1959 and came back to the United States where I stayed at Otis AFB in Massachusetts. That was where I was when I got word that my father passed away on March 28, 1960. I kind of went into shock. I was too stunned to cry. Phyllis stayed in Massachusetts with the children but I got emergency leave and flew home for my father's funeral and my entire family was there. There were a lot of tears. My mother took it the hardest. I didn't cry; I felt I had to be strong for the others, especially my mother. It was a very solemn day. I don't remember much of it. Again, I think I was in shock. My father's funeral ended and he was laid to rest. We all went home and stayed together for several somber days until we went back to our lives. I was surprised at how removed I had been. I figured the war had hardened me. I returned to Massachusetts and several weeks later, I was just walking down the street, when it hit me. My father was gone. The man who had made sacrifices for us his entire life; the man that worked morning, noon, and night, and scrimped and scraped to make sure his children all had college educations, was gone. I just completely broke down. I started sobbing and I couldn't stop. I had been walking down the street but I just stopped and sobbed silent tears in rivulets down my face. Countless images passed through my mind in a flash. My father's Christmas packages; the Sunday's spent with him at his work place; his smile; the loving way he held my mother; his calm, thoughtful manner; that knowing look he gave us when we were about to cross the line; a thousand memories from my childhood flashed before my streaming eyes. I had always known what my father had meant to my family, but it was magnified so much more so now that he was gone.

Just like during the war, when we had lost Sherman and Brooks, life went on. It was at Otis that my flight status was suspended in December of 1960. The Air Force was trying to save money. As a finance officer I didn't have to be a pilot anymore and the Air Corps wanted to cut down on flight pay.

I transferred to Selfridge AFB in Michigan in 1962 where I made lieutenant colonel. I retired from the Air Force August 23rd after 22 years of continuous active duty. I had had a very enjoyable time and a good career in the Army Air Corps and then United States Air Force. I think it was made easy for me because of my demeanor. I've always had a sense of humor and a quick wit. I had the ability to diffuse things. That doesn't mean I would take stuff. When it was time to speak up, I spoke up. I demanded the respect that came with my rank, but I also knew there were some things I just couldn't do anything about. Yet all through my military service, I was fortunate to have my base commanders always back me. I was lucky, but I think it was also because I picked my battles wisely. For instance, at Freeman Field I refused to sign the order as it was written and only signed it after I made my own amendment.

A career officer can't get something on his record. If a person can't get along with others, he will have problems. I think that worked both ways. I was known to be cool and level-headed. If someone didn't get along with me, that was noticed. The commander would wonder, "Why doesn't he get along with Jamison. Everyone else does." I always had a good record and a good reputation.

I served my country in two wars as a fighter pilot, a bomber pilot, a flying safety and accident investigating officer, and an accounting and finance officer at bases throughout the U.S., Asia, Europe and Africa. I maintained my active flight status and achieved a command pilot rating with more than 3000 hours. I served my country for twenty-two years.

Civilian Life

After my retirement in 1963 I went into the banking industry for a few years before returning to government service with the Social Security Administration. Starting as a claims representative, I moved on to hold positions as a field representative and branch manager. I moved back to Cleveland and that was where I was when my mother passed away in 1965. There were so many tears from the rest of my family and my children that, again, I had to be strong for the others. Standing over my mother, with both of my parents now laid to rest, I reflected on how lucky I had been to have such wonderful parents. My mother and father had taught us so much. They had taught us moral strength; dignity; the importance of work ethic; they had taught us that family always came first; that education was an absolute, and that excellence was expected. With my mother laid to rest beside my father, I knew that God had been very good to my family.

In 1972 I was selected to open and head one of the first metropolitan answering services in the nation, the precursor to today's tele-service centers.

My brother Thurston retired as a lieutenant colonel. He had fought with the 366th Infantry in Italy in the 92nd Division – an all black division. My other brother, Sterling, was also in the service during the war. He was the first of my siblings to pass away. Sterling served in the Pacific where he got Malaria. It wore him down and eventually killed him. My sister Rae Edwina Jamison became a schoolteacher. My younger brother Richard Henry Jamison Jr. was a principal at an elementary school. My youngest brother Alvin Rolland Jamison became a jet pilot. One of my old buddies from Tuskegee trained him at Williams's field.

When Alvin was in training, he was having a hard time with his takeoffs. He called me for advice. I told him, "You make that airplane go straight. Make it do what you want to do." He would over-think things, being too mechanical. He was having trouble keeping the nose straight on take offs. I told him, "You point that plane straight ahead and you make the plane go straight. You push that damn rudder as hard as you have too but you MAKE that plane go where you want it to go—straight ahead!" Later, he told me my advice really helped him." He was at Ellis Air force base in Nevada and his squadron flew F16's to Germany, the first time that an entire fighter squadron flew to Europe in formation. One of my buddies from Tuskegee, Leroy Roberts, was Alvin's flight leader. It was a small world. I was proud of my little brother; I was proud of all of my siblings.

In 1992 my Kidney's failed. I underwent dialysis and was told I would have to go through Kidney dialysis three times a week for the rest of my life. The doctors told me I had five years to live, tops, and probably less. I did not tell Phyllis but

153

knowing I was going to die, I made every preparation to make sure my wife was well off financially. I made all the arrangements for my death and felt satisfied that Phyllis would be okay. Then, in 1995, Phyllis passed away unexpectedly. I went into shock. How could that happen? I was supposed to die, not Phyllis. My world was completely upended. Phyllis had meant more to me than anyone. Phyllis had been to me what my mother had been to my father. I had survived the war. I had flown combat mission after mission. I had survived so many close calls during the war and flying. How could I outlive my wife? Phyllis was supposed to outlive me. She was the best wife; the best mother; she was a wonderful educator. She had meant so much to me and to so many people. She had stood by me and been the matriarch of our family. Now she was gone. Now I was alone after 53 years of marriage. I was in shock. But, as I had learned all throughout the war…life goes on.

Our two children, Michal and Clarence Clifford Jr., have both married and given me four grandchildren. Michal has a son and Clarence Clifford has three daughters. Celeste graduated from Hampton and got her Masters and PHD from Johns Hopkins University; Christine got a Masters at Kent State University and teaches in Warrensville Heights, Ohio; and Courtney is at Duke on a full scholarship. Education is still very important in the Jamison household.

Clarence Clifford graduated from Hampton University in Virginia and now works for Dupont, the chemical company. He travels the world as a civilian worker having been to the Far East including Japan, China, Singapore, Hong Kong and many other places.

Michal graduated from Vassar University in Poughkeepsie, New York, and is now retired, having worked as a management official for the Social Security Administration.

I am retired and live alone in Shaker Heights, Ohio. I travel the country from time to time, doing interviews for PBS, the History Channel, and other documentary shows. People often ask me the same question: How could you fly for a country that treated your people so poorly? I answer, "I knew I was a part of something special. There were no blacks in the Army Air Corps. That's why I've always considered us pioneers. If we didn't strive to be better, how would we ever get better as individuals or as a people? We simply didn't dwell on the bad things. We looked at the challenge of doing a task that was tough, demanding, exciting, and fun. Something others thought we were incapable of doing. I never had any doubts about my ability. I knew I could fly. I knew I had the ability, the brains, and the background. I had the utmost confidence even though I knew flying was inherently dangerous. It was the airplane that would kill me. It didn't matter if I was black, white, or green. They were washing out good pilots of all colors and I wanted to succeed. The black community was proud of the 99th Pursuit squadron, too, and that meant a lot. There were other guys that were just as good (or better) but they didn't get the opportunity. I did and I was determined to make the best of it. Were we fighting two wars? Yes, but I never remember any of us talking about that. There was just a great camaraderie, knowing we were part of something extraordinary.

The war is long since over, but it is something I often think about. In 2006, we are all in our late 80's, but I stay in touch with my friends from the 99th Pursuit Squadron like Jack Rogers, Bill Campbell, Spann Watson, Charles Dryden [x] and some of the others. Even now, at age 88, I still dream of my younger days.

I have had a recurring dream about my friend Sherman White for the last 63 years. Sherman was my friend at the University of Chicago and we took the civilian pilot training program together before being accepted into the 99th. Sherman disappeared somewhere over Sicily, but no one knew the circumstances involving his death. We'd heard tales that he'd bailed out or crash-landed somewhere in the North Africa desert. In my dream he always shows up at my tent, back at our airfield in Tunis in 1943.

"Where the hell have you been?" I always ask.

He answers, "Been living with the Arabs."

Even after all these years, although its gone the moment I wake up, the relief I feel at knowing my friend is okay is wonderful.

ⁱ Some of my buddies still call me C.J. I'm 87 now and a few of my childhood friends are still alive even in 2004. They still call me C.J.

ⁱⁱ I cannot find the copy I made of the original letter. It has been lost over the years. This is what I wrote.

ⁱⁱⁱ It later became Tuskegee College and then Tuskegee University but in 1941 it was the Tuskegee institute.

^{iv} Years later a movie titled, "The Tuskegee Airmen" would show a cadet played by Lawrence Fishburne taking her up. In truth it hadn't been a cadet. It was Chief Anderson.

^v British pilots often came over on war bond drives or for demonstrations and other PR stuff.

^{vi} Though he only got his fourth in 1997 when President Clinton gave it to him in retirement.

^{vii} Larger even than the fleet assembled on June 6th 1944, almost a year later.

^{viii} I also sent her a letter but it was intercepted by sensors.

^{ix} As of the late 1990's people would still say to me "I remember when you would come in low to buzz the house to tell your wife to come pick you up."

^x Dryden will call me tomorrow on our sixty-fourth anniversary.

For Further reading about the famous TUSKEGEE AIRMEN

Cooper, Charlie and Cooper Ann. Tuskegee's Heroes: Featuring the Aviation Art of Roy La Grone, foreword by Benjamin O. Davis, Jr. Osceola, WI, Motorbooks , 1996.
Davis, Benjamin O. Benjamin O. Davis, Jr., American : an autobiography. New York, N.Y, Plume, 1992.
Dryden, Charles W. A-Train: Memoirs of a Tuskegee Airman. Tuscaloosa, AL, University of Alabama Press, 1997.
Francis, Charles E. The Tuskegee Airmen: the Men Who Changed a Nation.. 3rd, revised and enlarged. Boston, Branden Pub. Co., 1993. Earlier editions published in 1956 and1988.
Gillead, Le Roy F. The Tuskegee Experiment and Tuskegee Airmen 1939-1949.. San Francisco, [n.p.], 1994.
Hastie, William Henry. On Clipped Wings: The Story of Jim Crow in the Army Air Corps. New York, National Association for the Advancement of Colored People, [1943].
Holway, John. Red Tails, Black Wings: The Men of America's Black Air Force.. Las Cruces, NM, Yucca Tree, 1997.
Johnson, Hayden C. The Fighting 99th Air Squadron, 1941-1945. New York, Vantage Press, 1987..
McKissack, Pat and McKissack Fredrick. Red-Tail Angels: The Story of the Tuskegee Airmen of World War II.. New York, Walker and Co., 1995..
Osur, Alan M. Blacks in the Army Air Forces during World War II. New York, Arno Press, 1980.
Rose, Robert A. Lonely Eagles: The Story of America's Black Air Force in World War II.. Los Angeles, Tuskegee Airmen, Los Angeles Chapter, 1980.
Sandler, Stanley. Segregated Skies: All-Black Combat Squadrons of WW II.. Washington, DC, Smithsonian Institution, 1992.
Scott, Lawrence P. and Womack Willima M. Double V: The Civil Rights Struggle of the Tuskegee Airmen..East Lansing, Michigan State University Press, 1994.
Warren, James C. The Freeman Field Mutiny: A Tuskegee Airmen's Story. Vacaville, CA, Conyers, 1996.

About the Author

James Christ has traveled throughout Europe, Africa, and Asia, visiting battlesights from Normandy to Zululand and Pearl Harbor to Jerusalem. James Christ is currently working on additional books about the Second World War, present day Afghanistan, and Iraq. He lives in Phoenix, Arizona, and raises his two beloved sons Nolan and Trace.

For further reading by James Christ, read "Mission Raise Hell" about the U.S. Marines on Choiseul, Oct- Nov, 1943, and "Gavutu and Bloody Ridge" about the U.S. Marines on Gavutu and Guadalcanal, Aug-Sep 1942, both published by the Naval Institute.